TABLE OF CONTENTS

Unless otherwise indicated, all Scripture quotations are taken from the *King James Version* of the Bible. Scripture taken from the Holy Bible, New International Version. Copyright © 1973, 1978, 1984 International Bible Society. All rights reserved.

The Law Of Recognition
ISBN 1-56394-095-7/B-114
Copyright © 1999 by **MIKE MURDOCK**
All publishing rights belong exclusively to Wisdom International
Publisher/Editor: Deborah Murdock Johnson
Published by The Wisdom Center · 4051 Denton Hwy. · Ft. Worth, Texas 76117
1-888-WISDOM-1 (1-817-759-0300) · **Website: TheWisdomCenter.tv**

WHY I WROTE THIS BOOK

Ignorance Is Deadly.

Ignorance perpetuates disease, poverty and failure.

Ignorance produces constant loss in our lives.

I have walked the streets of Calcutta, India with the late, great missionary, Mark Buntain, and smelled the horrifying stench of ignorance. Human decay, heartache and tragedy always occur through the trap of ignorance.

I love *Wisdom.*

I love to observe uncommon progress and miraculous changes Wisdom always creates.

It invigorates me to observe those who reach for the Golden Key of Wisdom to unlock the door to uncommon success in their lives.

Small keys unlock Golden Doors.

Small changes can create great futures.

I have noticed throughout the years that life involves a collection of Laws and Principles. Discovering those Laws can radically change the course of your life...instantly...forever.

Years ago, I read a powerful book concerning visualization and the results of it in your life. When I began to work with the *Law of Visualization,* my energy, health and even the quality of my friendships changed. When I discovered the *Law of Words,* the powerful force of speaking your future into existence, I was changed forever.

When God began to birth the revelation of *The Law of Recognition,* I knew I had tapped into one of the most powerful, undiscovered secrets of life.

For two years I kept hearing an inner voice saying, *"Everything You Need Or Want Is Already In Your Life—Merely Awaiting Your Recognition Of It."*

I knew it contained a *secret,* a powerful *code,* a hidden *message* to my spirit.

But, I really did not know how it applied.

I have always been an observant person. I study and scrutinize anything close to me. I listen to others with complete focus.

But, that statement persisted—echoing in my spirit and heart.

Then, like a million suns bursting on the horizon...*I saw it.* Instantly, I saw this Law at work in every person around me.

I knew *why* the successful succeeded.

I knew *why* people around me had failed.

I knew *the force* behind uncommon and victorious success.

The Law of Recognition.

As I studied the Bible, the greatest book on earth, it was revealed and illuminated like never before. I reviewed my personal life. It was like a huge neon sign...*The Law of Recognition.*

Anything Unrecognized Becomes Uncelebrated.

Anything Uncelebrated Becomes Unrewarded.

Anything Unrewarded Eventually Exits Your Life.

I knew this Golden Law for Uncommon Success must be shared with every person I met for the rest of my life.

It can heal any wound within you.

It can unleash more enthusiasm than you have ever known.

It will force unhappy memories to die within you.

It will correct your focus, create a magnetism around you and cause those in high places to pursue your company and relationship.

This Law is the *missing link* you have searched for throughout your life.

It will move you from poverty to prosperity.

It will replace tears with laughter.

It will answer the questions buried within you for a lifetime.

This Law is the Golden Bridge to the greatest season of your life.

I desperately want to help you succeed.

That's why I wrote this book.

Mike Murdock

≈ 1 ≈

THE LAW OF RECOGNITION

Life Is Governed By Laws.

The Law of Promotion teaches—*You Can Only Be Promoted By Someone Whose Instructions You Have Followed.*

The Law of Reproduction indicates—*You Can Only Reproduce Something You Are.*

The Law of The Seed reveals—*Whatever You Have In Your Hand Will Create Anything You Want In Your Future.*

The Law of Recognition teaches—*Everything You Need In Your Life Is Already In Your Life Merely Awaiting Your Recognition Of It.*

There is something you are not seeing in your life today...and it could be costing you dearly.

The Pharisees did not recognize the divinity of Jesus. It cost them eternity, miracles and the joy of His presence. Jesus wept over it. "And when He was come near, He beheld the city, and wept over it, Saying, If thou hadst known, even thou, at least in this thy day, the things which belong unto thy peace! but now they are *hid from thine eyes*...because thou knewest not the time of thy visitation," (Luke 19:41-42, 44).

Spiritual People Do Not Always Cooperate With The Law Of Recognition. Jesus saw it in His own disciples. "Having eyes, see ye not? and having ears, hear ye not? and do ye not remember?" (Mark 8:18).

The Law Of Recognition Can Turn A Lifetime Of Failure Into Instant Success. An excellent example is one of the thieves hanging next to Jesus at the crucifixion. The first, who did not recognize Jesus as the Son of God, cursed and was lost for eternity. The second *recognized* the Christ and begging for forgiveness, received it (Luke 23:42-43).

The Law Of Recognition Activates The Laws Of Preservation And Promotion. David recognized the anointing on King Saul and *received* the kingship himself. However, King Saul refused to recognize the anointing of God on David, and *lost* the throne.

The Law Of Recognition Can Move You From Obscurity To Significance Within Twenty-four Hours. Zacchaeus, the evil tax collector, *recognized* that Jesus was the Christ. Jesus responded to that respect by having a meal in his home and changing his life forever.

The Law of Recognition is changing my life and ministry every single day.

I had searched diligently for a qualified manager for our staff of twenty-five persons. No one emerged who brought a sense of peace to my soul and spirit. One day, while praying in "The Secret Place," I presented God my list of qualifications—what I desired in a general manager.

"Those qualities are in your secretary," He said.

I explained to The Holy Spirit that she was

my secretary, not my manager.

The Holy Spirit spoke so quietly, "No, she is your *manager*. You have placed her in position as a secretary, but she is the manager with the qualities you have pursued and requested. Everything you just told Me that you wanted is already in *her*."

She had been involved in my ministry for several years. She was godly, wise and respectful. She had already been here, but I just did not *recognize* her as my manager.

I attempted to sell my home for two-and-a-half years. It simply would not sell. During that time, I kept hearing in my heart The Voice of The Spirit, "Everything you want is *already* here. Everything you want is *already* here." I had no idea what He really meant. You see, I wanted to sell it because I wanted to be close to water or have a view from a hillside.

One day, a friend was pouring an asphalt jogging trail around my yard.

"Why don't you have a fish pond here on your property?" he asked.

"About twelve years ago, I inquired about it. I was told that my yard is too small since it's only seven acres," I answered.

"Oh no! It is easy to place a fish pond here." He paused and continued, "Now, I don't know what we would do with all of the soil if we dug it up, but, we could pile all of the soil on the other side of the yard. You could place a little table or gazebo on top. That would enable you to look down and see your llamas, antelope and emus on the other side of your property. Just move all your animals down by the creek." I stood there stunned as he showed me what he could see in that section of my yard. At that time, animals were running everywhere and it was a flat piece of property.

"You know what would be wonderful? You could have some water fountains shooting water about 15 feet into the air. You would be able to hear the *waterfall* outside your bedroom window every day and night."

I could not believe what I was hearing.

I ended up with six fish ponds. Two contain catfish, one contains bass and perch and two others contain Japanese Koi, a kind of beautiful goldfish.

Seven water fountains keep the sound of water around my house twenty-four hours a day. Walking around my yard sounds like I am on the beach all the time. In fact, my father said a few weeks ago while eating breakfast with me in the gazebo, "Son, if I was going to take a vacation, I'd just as soon be right here as anywhere I know on earth."

Think about this. It is almost crazy. Those fish ponds have existed in this yard...for years and years and years. I did not see them. I never saw them. You see, *all I had to do was take the soil out of them!*

▶ Some of the greatest gifts of your life have not yet been recognized.
▶ God has put something close to you that you are not seeing.
▶ Failure to recognize the gift is costing you incredibly.

The unsaved do not recognize the goodness of God. Like fools, they are plunging along in life without joy and supernatural victory.

I read a true story many years ago. It affected me then and it continues to affect me today.

A young couple became obsessed with the pursuit of gold during the great gold rush of the late 1800's. They decided to sell their farm and everything they owned to go pan or search for gold. Failure after failure, they eventually ended up bankrupt in Europe. After many years, they decided to come back to America and visit their farm. However, when they arrived here, they could not get close to their farm because it was surrounded with security guards and surveillance equipment to protect it. It turned out that under their farmhouse was the *second largest gold reserve* in America...now controlled by the government.

The farm they sold to go search for gold held the second largest gold mine in North America. They simply did not *recognize* it.

The Law of Recognition is simple but explosive.

> ▶ Everything You Need Is Already In Your Life Merely Awaiting Your Recognition Of It.
> ▶ Anything Unrecognized Remains Uncelebrated By You.
> ▶ Anything You Refuse To Celebrate Eventually Exits Your Life...A Gift, A Miracle Or A Person.

Throughout this book, The Holy Spirit will speak to you. You will suddenly have explosive and illuminating insights to miracles He has placed within you and those near you. Pride can blind you forever. Humility can unleash the greatest flow of miracles you can imagine.

The Law of Recognition will work for the poor.
It did for Ruth with Boaz.

The Law of Recognition will work for the sick.
It did for the blind man who cried out to Jesus.

The Law of Recognition will work for you as
you allow and permit The Holy Spirit to speak
through this book to your heart today.

❧ 2 ❧

RECOGNITION OF THE VOICE OF THE HOLY SPIRIT

The Master Communicator Is The Holy Spirit.
Nobody talks more than The Holy Spirit. He even created the universe by His words. "Through faith we understand that the worlds were framed by the word of God, so that things which are seen were not made of things which do appear," (Hebrews 11:3).

The cry of Jesus was that the Church listen to The Spirit. "He that hath an ear, let him hear what the Spirit saith unto the churches," (Revelation 2:7, 11, 17, 29).

Jesus talks to the *Father* (John 14:16).

The Father talks to The *Holy Spirit* (John 16:13).

The Holy Spirit talks to *us* (Revelation 2:7).

The Holy Spirit intercedes for you daily. "Likewise the Spirit also helpeth our infirmities: for we know not what we should pray for as we ought: but the Spirit [Himself] maketh intercession for us with groanings which cannot be uttered...because He maketh intercession for the saints according to the will of God," (Romans 8:26-27).

8 Rewards For Recognizing The Voice Of The Spirit

1. The Holy Spirit Often Warns Us Of Impending Danger. A choice and valued friend of mine pastored a large church in Texas many years ago. I was stunned when I heard of his tragic death in an airplane crash. It left me baffled, confused and disappointed. One year later, I was eating supper with his widow who related a fascinating insight.

"Mike, the morning of the crash, my husband sat on the edge of the bed at 5:30 a.m. and spoke to me, 'Honey, something tells me I should not fly today'."

He made a decision to override *the still small Voice.* Perhaps his speaking engagement was urgent and the expectations of others weighed heavily on him. Whatever the reason, he chose to ignore The Voice. His death occurred within hours.

2. Recognition Of His Voice Could Stop Thousands Of Unnecessary Deaths, Tragedies And Difficulties. Many times, I have received reports of those who died untimely and unnecessary deaths. Over and over, it has come back that the person felt uneasy and reluctant to keep their plans, but did so...overriding the small Voice.

3. Recognition Of His Voice Could Avoid Many Broken Marriages And Homes. When I was nineteen years old, I fell in love. One night in the prayer room, I wept for hours over the relationship. The Holy Spirit spoke clearly, "I do not want you in this relationship. End it." After I ended it, some of my college professors confirmed that Voice by saying, "Mike, I think it's a wise decision that you and the young lady move separate directions."

Three weeks later, I overrode The Voice. I *returned* to the relationship.

Thirteen years later, while standing on the courthouse steps of Houston, Texas, after the divorce proceedings, The Holy Spirit reminded me gently, "I gave you the instruction over thirteen years ago."

4. Recognition Of His Voice Can Unlock Waves Of Favor And Blessing. One afternoon my kitchen telephone rang in Houston, Texas. It was a dear friend, Roger McDuff. Roger has been a legend in gospel music for many years.

"Mike, while shaving, The Holy Spirit spoke to me to ask you to go with me to California. Paul and Jan Crouch head Channel 40 in Santa Ana, California. Have you heard of them?"

I had not.

"If you can purchase your ticket, I would like to introduce you to them. I believe that there is a connection between you and them."

Within days, Paul Crouch invited me to be a continuous guest on scores and scores of programs. He and Jan sponsored my telecast on their station for over four years. Many miracles occurred. Thousands of people received our ministry. It was astounding.

Roger heard The Voice of The Spirit.

I heard The Voice of The Spirit.

Miracles have been a wave ever since then. I met some of the most wonderful people such as

Rosie Greer, Laverne Tripp, Dwight Thompson and many others.

5. The Voice Will Always Connect You With Uncommon People In Your Life.

6. Recognition Of His Voice Brings Inner Peace. It happened to the disciples during the storm while they were on the ship.

7. Recognition Of His Voice Unlocks Uncommon Prosperity. "And it shall come to pass, if thou shalt hearken diligently unto *the voice* of the Lord thy God, to observe and to do all His commandments which I command thee this day, that the Lord thy God will set thee on high above all nations of the earth: And all these *blessings shall come* on thee, and overtake thee, if thou shalt hearken unto the Voice of the Lord thy God," (Deuteronomy 28:1-2).

8. The Voice Of The Spirit Can Change The Financial Seasons Of Your Life In A Moment. My first year of evangelism was a financial catastrophe. One month my income was $35. Another month, it was $90. The first twelve months of evangelism, my income was $2,263. I owned a 1953 Chevrolet during my second year of evangelism, 1967. During the month of June, as I recall, I was invited to attend the South Texas District Council of the Assemblies of God. The speaker was Charles Greenaway, a beloved and respected missionary. He spoke and mentioned Leviticus 19:9 and 10. I had not noticed it before. I can almost hear him today...

"*How big is your corner?* In the Old Testament, the rich were instructed to leave the corners of their barley or wheat fields for the poor.

God promised to bless them if they would *sow* back and make their corners big to God and the people who were hurting." He continued, "Your field is your *income*. Your corners represent your *outgo* to God. If you will increase the size of your corners, God will increase the size of your field, or your income."

I do not recall ever hearing that philosophy before. It was an Assemblies of God missionary evangelist who told me that I could influence my financial income through returning a portion of it back to God.

Charles Greenaway was raising money for the missions department and encouraged us to make twelve-month faith promises. I was not familiar with this, but, I got inspired. While sitting there I decided I would "take a leap of faith."

He shouted, *"I dare you to prove God!* The only place God told you to prove His existence was in Malachi 3. He simply said to throw Him something up toward Heaven and if more came back than you threw up...that was the proof of His existence."

Something in me decided to believe.

Shaking, I stood to my feet. I made a $100 faith promise. I did so because they gave me twelve months to come up with $100. That was one-half of a month's income for me.

Driving back to Lake Charles, Louisiana, where I lived, was quite an emotional trip.

Where on earth was I going to find $100?

The house I was living in was purchased by my father for the grand total price of...$150! He had purchased the entire house for $150, and moved it on some land he had. So, I was living in it. My bedroom suite cost $35. I had purchased it from one of my father's deacons, Brother Stanley.

That was Thursday morning as I drove back from Victoria, Texas, to Lake Charles.

Sunday morning, an old pianist for the Stamps Quartet had dropped by our church. His name was Merle Daley. When he finished playing a piano solo for my father's church, he stood.

"Folks, God has been so good to me! Right now, my pockets are full of $100 bills!" I stared wide-eyed.

Suddenly, he looked at me sitting in the far-left seat of the building.

"In fact, God just spoke to me to give one of these $100 bills to Mike!"

I knew he knew God!

Monday morning, I deposited his gift of $100 in my checking account and promptly wrote a check to the South Texas District Council of the Assemblies of God to pay my faith promise.

Tuesday morning, I drove to Beeville, Texas, to minister at the First Assembly of God Church where James Brothers was host pastor. While driving through Beeville, I saw a small trailer with a "FOR SALE" sign on it of $100. It was precisely the very kind of trailer I had been wanting to bring my clothes, books and belongings around to the meetings. I was sick inside because I had paid my faith promise...and *no longer had the $100 to purchase the little trailer.* It seemed to me that satan whispered to my heart, "See what you could have had if you had not paid your faith promise!" I agreed, of course.

That night, I went early to the church and sat at the old upright piano on the platform. While practicing before service, a couple walked in. In a few minutes, she walked up behind me at the piano and tapped me on the shoulder.

"My husband and I felt impressed to give this to you."

I turned around and looked at one of the most beautiful sights I have ever seen—her check for $150!

"This is God, my Sister! I saw a small trailer today while driving through town that I have desperately wanted that cost $100. Now I have more than enough to buy it!" I exclaimed with joy.

The next day, Wednesday, I purchased the trailer and had $50 left over. So, I immediately rushed another Seed of $50 to the South Texas District Council Assemblies of God Office in Houston. I had already paid my faith promise, but I felt that anything that works that good that fast...I was determined to work the living daylights out of!

Wednesday night came. While I was practicing the piano again, the couple walked in. Again, she approached me with another beautiful check.

"We could not sleep last night. The Holy Spirit spoke to our hearts and said we were supposed to buy this trailer for you also. Here's another check for $100 to pay for the trailer."

My miracle parade of Harvests had just been birthed.

His still small Voice had activated a collection of miracles that would change my life forever.

When Any Minister Of God Speaks Under The Anointing, You Are Hearing The Voice Of The Holy Spirit. "Believe in the Lord your God, so shall ye be established; believe His prophets, so shall ye prosper," (2 Chronicles 20:20).

When Your Conscience Feels Convicted, You Are Hearing The Voice Of The Spirit. "And when He is come, He will reprove the world of sin, and of righteousness, and of judgment," (John 16:8).

When You Read The Word Of God, You Are Hearing The Voice Of The Spirit. "All scripture is given by inspiration of God, and is profitable for doctrine, for reproof, for correction, for instruction in righteousness," (2 Timothy 3:16).

The Most Important Thing In Your Life Is Recognition Of The Voice Of The Holy Spirit.

His Voice is the only Voice that truly matters.

Nobody can talk to God for you.

Nobody can *know* The Voice of God for you. That's why the psalmist cried, "O God, Thou art my God; early will I seek Thee: my soul thirsteth for Thee, my flesh longeth for Thee in a dry and thirsty land, where no water is; To see Thy power and Thy glory, so as I have seen Thee in the sanctuary," (Psalm 63:1-2).

What You Hear First Determines What You Will Speak Next.

Listen to His Voice before you listen to the needs of your own family. You see, His Voice will produce the confidence you need to provide for your family.

Listen to His Voice before your doctor enters the room with news of unbelief and doubt.

Listen to His Voice before others have an

opportunity to affect you.

Listen to His Voice instead of the critical words of others who desire to break your focus and destroy your self-confidence.

Listen to His Voice and your attitude will change miraculously to faith and new victory and hope.

Listen to His Voice before you listen to the voice of doubters. Your faith is the gate to your future.

Listen to His Voice before you listen to the ideas and suggestions of those near you. Ideas are not commands.

Listen to His Voice before you make any commitment to men of your time, money or enthusiasm.

Listen to His Voice before you make any dramatic or significant changes in your life or ministry.

Recognition of His Voice enables you to know your Assignment, discern the pitfalls and unleash your faith for the next season of achievement in your life.

12 Facts You Should Know About The Holy Spirit

1. **The Holy Spirit Is A Person, Not Fire, Wind Or A White Dove.** "And I will pray the Father, and He shall give you another Comforter, that He may abide with you for ever," (John 14:16).

2. **The Holy Spirit Created You.** "The Spirit of God hath made me, and the breath of the Almighty hath given me life," (Job 33:4). The Apostle Paul wrote, "But the Spirit giveth life," (2 Corinthians 3:6).

Jesus taught it. "The Spirit gives life," (John 6:63 NIV).

3. The Holy Spirit Authored The Word Of God. "For the prophecy came not in old time by the will of man: but holy men of God spake as they were moved by the Holy Ghost," (2 Peter 1:21).

The Apostle Paul taught it. "All scripture is given by inspiration of God, and is profitable for doctrine, for reproof, for correction, for instruction in righteousness: That the man of God may be perfect, throughly furnished unto all good works," (2 Timothy 3:16-17).

4. The Holy Spirit Selects The Gifts And Skills Given To You By The Father. "Now there are diversities of gifts, but the same Spirit. And there are differences of administrations, but the same Lord. For to one is given by the Spirit the word of wisdom; to another the word of knowledge by the same Spirit; To another faith by the same Spirit; to another the gifts of healing by the same Spirit," (1 Corinthians 12:4-5, 8-9).

5. The Holy Spirit Determines To Whom You Are Assigned, For A Moment, Or Your Lifetime. "Then the Spirit said unto Philip, Go near, and join thyself to this chariot," (Acts 8:29).

6. The Holy Spirit Knows The Geographical Location Where Your Gifts Will Flourish And Be Celebrated. "So they, being sent forth by the Holy Ghost, departed unto Seleucia; and from thence they sailed to Cyprus," (Acts 13:4).

7. The Holy Spirit Births An Uncommon Love For Those To Whom You Are Called.

"Because the love of God is shed abroad in our hearts by the Holy Ghost which is given unto us," (Romans 5:5).

8. The Holy Spirit Is Pleasured By Singing And Worship. "The Lord thy God in the midst of thee is mighty; He will save, He will rejoice over thee with joy; He will rest in His love, He will joy over thee with singing," (Zephaniah 3:17).

His Rules of Conduct include entering His presence with singing. "Come before His presence with singing," (Psalm 100:2).

9. The Holy Spirit Intercedes For You Every Moment. "Likewise the Spirit also helpeth our infirmities...but the Spirit [Himself] maketh intercession for us with groanings which cannot be uttered," (Romans 8:26).

10. The Holy Spirit Is Easily Offended. "Let no corrupt communication proceed out of your mouth, but that which is good to the use of edifying, that it may minister grace unto the hearers. And grieve not the Holy Spirit of God, whereby ye are sealed unto the day of redemption. Let all bitterness, and wrath, and anger, and clamour, and evil speaking, be put away from you, with all malice: And be ye kind one to another, tenderhearted, forgiving one another, even as God for Christ's sake hath forgiven you," (Ephesians 4:29-32).

11. When The Holy Spirit Is Offended, He Withdraws His Manifest Presence. "I will go and return to My place, till they acknowledge their offence, and seek My face: in their affliction they will seek Me early," (Hosea 5:15). Depression is the proof of His withdrawal.

12. Joy Is The Proof The Holy Spirit Is Present. "In Thy presence is fulness of joy; at Thy right hand there are pleasures for evermore," (Psalm 16:11).

The greatest discovery of my lifetime is the habitual companionship of The Holy Spirit, The One Who Stayed.

Recognition Of The Voice Of The Holy Spirit Is The Master Secret Of Life.

RECOMMENDED BOOKS AND TAPES ON THIS TOPIC

B-23   Seeds of Wisdom on Prayer (32 pages/$3)
B-100   The Holy Spirit Handbook (153 pages/$10)
B-101   The 3 Most Important Things In Your Life (240 pages/$10)
B-115   Seeds of Wisdom on The Secret Place (32 pages/$5)
TS-08   The Strategy of Hourly Obedience (6 tapes/$30)
TS-29   The Holy Spirit Handbook (6 tapes/$30)
TS-59   Love Songs to The Holy Spirit (6 tapes/$30)

≈ 3 ≈

RECOGNITION OF YOUR ASSIGNMENT

You Are Here On Assignment.

Everything God created is a solution to a problem. Your eyes see. Your ears hear. Mothers solve emotional problems. Dentists solve teeth problems. Lawyers solve legal problems.

Your Assignment on the earth is to solve a problem for somebody, somewhere and receive a reward for it. "Let every man abide in the same calling wherein he was called," (1 Corinthians 7:20).

When your Assignment is unrecognized, you are uncelebrated. When you are not celebrated, you are not rewarded. *No Torment On Earth Equals The Torment Of Living A Life Unrewarded For The Gift And Solution Lying Dormant Within You.*

10 Facts You Must Know About Your Assignment

1. Your Assignment Is Always To A Person Or A People. "...for thou shalt go to all that I shall send thee, and whatsoever I command thee thou shalt speak," (Jeremiah 1:7).

Paul understood this. "Whereunto I am appointed a preacher, and an apostle, and a teacher of the Gentiles," (2 Timothy 1:11).

2. Your Assignment Determines The Suffering And Attacks You Encounter. When Paul described his appointment as a preacher and teacher, he explained this. "For the which cause I also suffer these things: nevertheless I am not ashamed: for I know Whom I have believed, and am persuaded that He is able to keep that which I have committed unto Him against that day," (2 Timothy 1:12).

3. What Grieves You Is A Clue To What You Are Assigned To Heal And Restore. Nehemiah understood this. "...the wall of Jerusalem also is broken down, and the gates thereof are burned with fire. And it came to pass, when I heard these words, that I sat down and wept, and mourned certain days, and fasted, and prayed before the God of heaven," (Nehemiah 1:3-4). Compassion is always a signpost to the geographical location where you belong. What makes you *cry* is a clue to the problem God has qualified you to *heal*.

4. What You Love The Most Reveals The Greatest Gifts You Contain. Passion is the path to your Wisdom. When I know what you love to *talk* about, *think* about and *learn* about—that is your place of Assignment. You will only have Wisdom for something you love.

What do you love the most?

The Proof Of Love Is The Investment Of Time.

When I find where you are willing to invest your *time*, I know what you *love*. That is your

Assignment. That is why Moses was willing to counsel with people from daylight to dark—he loved his people with all his heart (read Exodus 18:13-14).

5. Your Assignment Is Geographical. Where you are matters as much as what you are. You may be a beautiful whale—but, you better be in water! Geography matters. It controls the flow of favor in your life.

Who Sees You Determines Who Promotes You.

You will rarely receive favor unless someone *sees* you. Geography affects the increase of favor. That's why Jesus taught to go where you are *celebrated* instead of where you are *tolerated*. Abraham left his father's house. Ruth left Moab and followed Naomi back to Bethlehem. *Geography* plays a major part in every success story (read Deuteronomy 12:14, 26).

6. You Will Only Succeed When Your Assignment Becomes An Obsession. That explains the Apostle Paul's uncommon achievement. "This *one thing* I do, forgetting those things which are behind, and reaching forth unto those things which are before, I press toward *the mark* for the prize of the high calling of God in Christ Jesus," (Philppians 3:13-14).

7. Your Assignment Will Require Seasons Of Preparation. "Study to shew thyself approved unto God, a workman that needeth not to be ashamed, rightly dividing the Word of truth," (2 Timothy 2:15). You will experience seasons of insignificance, isolation, waiting, warfare, persecution, injustice, silence and promotion. Jesus invested 30 years of preparation for three-

and-one-half years of ministry (see Luke 3:23).

8. Your Assignment May Be Misunderstood By Your Own Family And Those Closest To You. Jesus experienced this. "For neither did His brethren believe in Him," (John 7:5). Stay aware of your difference from others. *God provides your family to prepare you for an enemy.* Everything in your future is already in your present house, Judas or Doubting Thomas! *Your family is your School.*

Your family wants you *humbled.*

Your enemy wants you *destroyed.*

Your survival of your family is proof you will survive your future as well!

9. Your Assignment Will Always Have An Enemy. The servant is not above his lord. Jesus declared it. "If the world hate you, ye know that it hated Me before it hated you...The servant is not greater than his lord. If they have persecuted Me, they will also persecute you," (John 15:18, 20-21). Your enemies are as necessary as your friends.

Your friends provide *comfort.*

Your enemy provides *promotion.*

Enemies turn nobodies into somebodies. *The only difference between obscurity and significance is the enemy you decide to conquer.* Without Goliath, David would remain hidden without significance in the pages of history as a shepherd boy on a hillside. (See chapter 19 on *"Recognition Of The Enemy God Will Use To Promote You."*)

10. Your Assignment Is The Only Place Your Financial Provision Is Guaranteed. God instructed Elijah to go to the brook where a raven would feed him (read 1 Kings 17). There, he received his daily provision. One day, the brook dried up. Why? His Assignment had *changed*.

Lack is a clue that God is changing your Assignment. Elijah's new Assignment was to visit Zarephath, where a starving widow would receive her financial miracle throughout the remaining part of the famine. When God sends you to a place, provision is the promised incentive for obedience.

Thousands are discovering their Assignment throughout the earth these days. Their joy is exploding. Their peace is like a glory cloud around their life. Depression leaves. Fear dissipates. Uncommon favor enters their life daily because they are at their place of Assignment.

Recognizing Your Assignment Will Dry Your Tears, Unload Your Burdens And Restore The Joy To Your Countenance.

RECOMMENDED BOOKS AND TAPES ON THIS TOPIC

B-12   The Minister's Encyclopedia, 3 Vols. (890 pages/$90)
B-44   31 Secrets for Career Success (114 pages/$10)
B-74   The Assignment: The Dream & The Destiny, Vol. 1 (164 pages/$10)
B-75   The Assignment: The Anointing & The Adversity, Vol. 2 (192 pages/$10)
B-97   The Assignment: The Trials & The Triumphs, Vol. 3 (160 pages/$10)
B-98   The Assignment: The Pain & The Passion, Vol. 4 (144 pages/$10)
B-107 The Uncommon Minister, Vol. 1 (32 pages/$5)
B-108 The Uncommon Minister, Vol. 2 (32 pages/$5)
B-109 The Uncommon Minister, Vol. 3 (32 pages/$5)
B-110 The Uncommon Minister, Vol. 4 (32 pages/$5)
B-111 The Uncommon Minister, Vol. 5 (32 pages/$5)
B-112 The Uncommon Minister, Vol. 6 (32 pages/$5)
B-113 The Uncommon Minister, Vol. 7 (32 pages/$5)
TS-02 The Grasshopper Complex (6 tapes/$30)
TS-03 How to Walk Through Fire (6 tapes/$30)
TS-08 The Strategy of Hourly Obedience (6 tapes/$30)
TS-24 31 Secrets of The Uncommon Problem Solver (6 tapes/$30)
TS-52 The Assignment: The Dream & The Destiny (6 tapes/$30)

"When wisdom entered into thine heart, and knowledge is pleasant unto thy soul; Discretion shall preserve thee, understanding shall keep thee: to deliver thee from the way of the evil man, from the man that speaketh froward things; Who leave the paths of uprightness, to walk in the ways of darkness;...Where no counsel is, the people fall: but in the multitude of counselors there is safety."
Proverbs 4:10-13; 11:14

∾ 4 ∾

RECOGNITION OF AN UNCOMMON MENTOR

Mentors Are Teachers Of Wisdom.
Various Mentors will enter and exit your life. The Holy Spirit is your dominant and most important Mentor of all (see John 14:15-16).
Wisdom determines the success of your life.
There are two ways to receive Wisdom:
1. Mistakes
2. Mentors
Mentors are the difference between poverty and prosperity; decrease and increase; loss and gain; pain and pleasure; deterioration and restoration.

12 Facts You Should Know About An Uncommon Mentor

1. An Uncommon Mentor Is The Master Key To The Success Of A Protegé. "Wisdom is the principal thing," (Proverbs 4:7).

2. An Uncommon Mentor Transfers Wisdom Through Relationship. "He that walketh with wise men shall be wise: but a companion of fools shall be destroyed," (Proverbs 13:20). Joshua knew this. "And Joshua the son of

Nun was full of the spirit of wisdom; for Moses had laid his hands upon him," (Deuteronomy 34:9).

3. An Uncommon Mentor Guarantees Your Promotion. "Exalt her, and she shall promote thee: she shall bring thee to honour, when thou dost embrace her. She shall give to thine head an ornament of grace: a crown of glory shall she deliver to thee," (Proverbs 4:8-9).

4. An Uncommon Mentor Can Determine Your Wealth. "Riches and honour are with Me; yea, durable riches and righteousness," (Proverbs 8:18).

5. An Uncommon Mentor Can Paralyze Your Enemies Against You. "For I will give you a mouth and wisdom, which all your adversaries shall not be able to gainsay nor resist," (Luke 21:15).

6. An Uncommon Mentor Can Cause Influential People To Listen To You. "And Joshua the son of Nun was full of the spirit of wisdom; for Moses had laid his hands upon him: and *the children of Israel hearkened unto him,*" (Deuteronomy 34:9).

7. An Uncommon Mentor Will Require Your Pursuit. He does not need what you know. You need what he knows. Elijah never pursued Elisha. Elisha desired what was in him. *The Proof Of Desire Is Pursuit.*

8. An Uncommon Mentor Is More Interested In Your Success Than Your Affection. His focus is not the celebration of you, but, the correction of you.

9. An Uncommon Mentor Is Not

Necessarily Your Best Friend. Your best friend loves you the way you are. Your Mentor loves you too much to leave you the way you are.

Your Best Friend is comfortable with your *past*.

Your Mentor is comfortable with your *future*.
Your Best Friend *ignores* your weakness.
Your Mentor *removes* your weakness.
Your Best Friend is your *cheerleader*.
Your Mentor is your *coach*.
Your Best Friend sees what you do *right*.
Your Mentor sees what you do *wrong*.

10. An Uncommon Mentor Sees Things You Cannot See. He sees weaknesses in you before you experience the pain of them. He sees an enemy before you discern him. He has already experienced the pain of a problem you are about to create.

11. An Uncommon Mentor Will Become An Enemy To The Enemies Of His Protegé. Jesus proved this. "Simon, Simon, behold, satan hath desired to have you, that he may sift you as wheat: But I have prayed for thee, that thy faith fail not: and when thou art converted, strengthen thy brethren," (Luke 22:31-32). An uncommon Mentor will fight against any philosophy, pitfalls or prejudices that would rob the protegé of experiencing complete success in his life.

12. An Uncommon Mentor Can Create An Uncommon Protegé. Jesus took a fisherman and turned Peter into a master preacher. Everything you know will come through Mentorship, by experience or a person.

Invest everything to spend time and moments with an uncommon Mentor God has chosen to sow into your life.

Recognition Of An Uncommon Mentor Will Prevent A Thousand Heartaches.

RECOMMENDED BOOKS AND TAPES ON THIS TOPIC

B-44   31 Secrets for Career Success (114 pages/$10)
B-91   The Leadership Secrets of Jesus (196 pages/$10)
B-99   Secrets of the Richest Man Who Ever Lived (179 pages/$10)
B-104 7 Keys to 1000 Times More (128 pages/$10)
TS-06 Secrets of the Greatest Achievers Who Ever Lived, Series 1 (6 tapes/$30)
TS-07 Secrets of the Greatest Achievers Who Ever Lived, Series 2 (6 tapes/$30)
TS-25 Secrets of the Richest Man Who Ever Lived (6 tapes/$30)
TS-37 31 Secrets of an Uncommon Mentor (6 tapes/$30)

∾ 5 ∾

RECOGNITION OF AN UNCOMMON PROTEGÉ

A Protegé Is An Enthusiastic Learner.
The Wisdom of the Mentor is perpetuated through the Protegé. As I have said for many years, true success will produce a Successor. Jesus took twelve Protegés and revolutionized the earth.

It is very important that you recognize those connected to you by The Holy Spirit for the multiplying and perpetuation of your success and life.

You will only remember what you teach another. Our children should become our Protegés.

Passive Protegés only reach when it is convenient or when their personal efforts do not produce their desired result. They subconsciously expect their Mentor to produce success for them.

Parasite Protegés pursue for credibility, not correction. They will use the name and influence of a Mentor to manipulate others into a relationship. They want what the Mentor has *earned,* not what he has learned. They want reputation *without* preparation.

Prodigal Protegés enter and exit the relationship freely. When serious correction occurs, they move toward another Mentor who has not yet discovered their flaws. They distance themselves when their Mentor encounters personal difficulties, loss of credibility or false accusation or persecution. They only return when their pigpen becomes unbearable.

Productive Protegés are uncommon. They have a servant's heart. They never make a major decision without the counsel and feedback of their Mentor. They view their Mentor as a dominant gift from God. They love their Mentor as much as themselves.

The Uncommon Protegé assigned by God will honor the Mentor. "And we beseech you, brethren, to know them which labour among you, and are over you in the Lord, and admonish you; And to esteem them very highly in love for their work's sake," (1 Thessalonians 5:12-13).

9 Facts About The Uncommon Protegé

1. The Uncommon Protegé Will Invest Everything To Stay In The Presence Of The Uncommon Mentor. Ruth persisted. "Intreat me not to leave thee, or to return from following after thee: for whither thou goest, I will go," (Ruth 1:16).

2. The Uncommon Protegé Follows The Counsel Of The Uncommon Mentor. God established the punishment of a rebellious Protegé who sneered at the counsel of his covering. "And the man that will do presumptuously, and will not hearken unto the priest that standeth to minister there before the Lord thy God, or unto the judge, even that man shall die: and thou shalt put away the evil from Israel. And all the people shall hear, and fear, and do no more presumptuously," (Deuteronomy 17:12-13).

3. The Uncommon Protegé Reveals The Secrets And Dreams Of His Heart With The Mentor. Ruth opened her heart to Naomi. Elisha expressed his longings to Elijah. Vulnerability creates the unbreakable bond between a Mentor and the Protegé.

4. The Uncommon Protegé Freely Discusses His Mistakes And Pain With The Mentor. David did. "So David fled, and escaped, and came to Samuel to Ramah, and told him all that Saul had done to him. And he and Samuel went and dwelt in Naioth," (1 Samuel 19:18).

5. The Uncommon Protegé Defines Clearly His Expectations To The Mentor. Elisha explained his desire to Elijah. Ruth explained her desire to Naomi.

6. The Uncommon Protegé Gladly Sows Seeds Of Appreciation Back Into The Life Of The Mentor. It was the secret of the queen of Sheba. She presented over four million dollars of gifts when she met Solomon for the appointment. "And she came to Jerusalem with a very great train, with camels that bare spices, and very much gold, and precious stones: and when she was come to Solomon, she communed with him of all that was in her heart. And Solomon told her all her questions: there was not any thing hid from the king, which he told her not...And she gave the king an hundred and twenty talents of gold, and of spices very great store, and precious stones: there came no more such abundance of spices as these which the queen of Sheba gave to king Solomon," (1 Kings 10:2-3, 10).

The remarkable Mentor, the Apostle Paul, received such gifts. "For even in Thessalonica ye

sent once and again unto my necessity,"
(Philippians 4:16).

   7. **The Uncommon Protegé Ultimately
Receives The Mantle Of The Mentor He
Serves.** Transference of anointing is a fact, not a
fantasy. The Apostle Paul documented it.
"Wherefore I put thee in remembrance that thou
stir up the gift of God, which is in thee by the
putting on of *my hands,*" (2 Timothy 1:6).

   Joshua received it. "There shall not any man
be able to stand before thee all the days of thy life:
as I was with Moses, so I will be with thee: I will
not fail thee, nor forsake thee," (Joshua 1:5).

   8. **The Uncommon Protegé Moves
Toward The Shelter Of The Mentor During A
Season Of Uncommon Attack And Warfare.**
The picture of David and Samuel's relationship is
remarkable. "So David fled, and escaped, and came
to Samuel to Ramah, and told him all that Saul
had done to him. And he and Samuel went and
dwelt in Naioth," (1 Samuel 19:18). Think about
this seriously. During serious attack, David did
not withdraw from Samuel. He pursued him. He
invested *time* with him.

   9. **The Uncommon Protegé Will Change
His Own Schedule To Invest Time In The
Presence Of The Mentor.** Paul did. "Neither
went I up to Jerusalem to them which were
apostles before me; but I went into Arabia, and
returned again unto Damascus. Then after three
years I went up to Jerusalem to see Peter, and
abode with him fifteen days," (Galatians 1:17-18).

   The Uncommon Protegé is someone who
discerns, respects and pursues the answers God
has stored in The Mentor for their life.

What To Do When The Mentor/Protegé Relationship Is Threatened

Satan despises unity.

He fears the Law of Agreement. He will invest everything to destroy the transference of Wisdom.

Mentors are heartbroken when a worthy Protegé withdraws. I am certain Paul was heartbroken over Demas forsaking him. The father was heartbroken at the departure of the prodigal son. Jesus wept over Jerusalem (read Matthew 23).

Here are some thoughts that have helped me when a Protegé withdraws:

▶ You cannot *force* someone to learn from you. Jesus Himself could not and neither can you.

▶ There is usually a third party that destroys the unity between The Mentor and The Protegé. Unless The Protegé opens his heart about it, you cannot correct it.

▶ You cannot answer questions The Protegé refuses to ask.

▶ You cannot help anyone who feels you are unqualified to bring increase into their life.

▶ Protegés withdraw when they believe their own goals are superior to the goals of The Mentor.

▶ Protegés become discouraged by The Mentor's expressed disappointment in them.

▶ When the counsel of The Mentor is rejected, God will correct them through painful experiences.

▶ The Law of Repetition is necessary in the learning process.

Oral Roberts said, "When *you* get sick and tired of saying what you're saying, *you* are just then beginning to get it *yourself.* When your *staff* becomes sick and tired of hearing you teach something, *they* are just then beginning to get it *themselves.* And, when your people become sick and tired of hearing you say something, *they* are just then beginning to understand it."

▶ The Protegé is not necessarily the confidante of The Mentor.

▶ Questions should be addressed to The Mentor.

▶ Answers should be addressed to The Protegé.

The Greatest Success Quality Known Is The Willingness To Become.

Recognition Of An Uncommon Protégé Will Create An Inner Contentment No Other Achievement Can Produce.

RECOMMENDED BOOKS AND TAPES ON THIS TOPIC

B-14   Seeds of Wisdom on Relationships (32 pages/$3)
B-44   31 Secrets for Career Success (114 pages/$10)
B-58   The Mentor's Manna on Attitude (32 pages/$3)
B-71   Wisdom-God's Golden Key to Success (67 pages/$7)
B-85   The Gift of Wisdom for Teenagers (32 pages/$10)
B-91   The Leadership Secrets of Jesus (196 pages/$10)
B-99   Secrets of the Richest Man Who Ever Lived (179 pages/$10)
TS-06   Secrets of the Greatest Achievers Who Ever Lived, Series 1 (6 tapes/$30)
TS-07   Secrets of the Greatest Achievers Who Ever Lived, Series 2 (6 tapes/$30)
TS-25   Secrets of the Richest Man Who Ever Lived (6 tapes/$30)

❧ 6 ❧

RECOGNITION OF THE MATE GOD HAS APPROVED FOR YOU

You Are Designed For Connection.
Eyes require a view. Ears require sound. The mind requires thoughts.

Aloneness creates vulnerability. God knew it. "And the Lord God said, It is not good that the man should be alone," (Genesis 2:18).

God loves marriage. He hates divorce. Marriage is not a mere reproduction center for human babies.

Marriage is sowing ground where you sow your patience, love and enthusiasm, and watch it multiply in those around you who celebrate your presence.

God Will Never Give You A Gift That Will Replace His Presence. That is why a mate is not designed to produce your joy. The presence of God creates your joy. "In Thy presence is fulness of joy," (Psalm 16:11). Fullness implies "requiring nothing in addition."

Your mate is a gift from God to you. That gift is intended to: 1) protect your focus, 2) reduce distractions, and 3) create a climate of protection.

Focus often creates blindness. When you are looking north, you cannot see south. Someone else is needed for your protection. So, God provides the gift of a Mate.

Unfortunately, some who qualify for our attention are often unqualified to receive our heart.

Having been single for the last 20 years, I have had 2 decades to meditate, observe and analyze the failures and successes of relationships.

Here are some suggestions from two books I am writing: 1) *Think Twice Before Marrying Him* and 2) *Think Twice Before Marrying Her.*

1. Think Twice If You Do Not Possess A Passionate Desire To Give To Them. The Proof Of Love Is The Desire To Give. Jesus explained it. "For God so loved the world, that He *gave* His only begotten Son," (John 3:16).

Too often, marriage becomes an exchange. Exchange is the evidence of business, not love.

You should desire to give Time, the greatest gift God gave you.

The Proof Of Uncommon Love Is The Investment Of Time.

2. Think Twice If They Do Not Possess A Passionate Desire To Give Back To You. I am not referring to expensive gifts, huge amounts of money or clothes. A listening ear, flexibility, patience and the willingness to be corrected are gifts.

3. Think Twice If Your Personal Achievements Do Not Create Excitement In Them. When good things happen, who is the first person you desire to telephone? Pay attention to that.

Celebration Is A Compass. Those you love to celebrate with are clues to the puzzle of your life. When uncommon love exists, uncommon celebration is normal. Uncommon love does not compete with the success of another. It tastes and savors and enjoys the pleasure of another.

4. Think Twice If They Have Not Been Captivated By What Has Captivated You. Several years ago, a lady excited me. Yet, the relationship struggled. Something simply could not seem to "catch fire." She did not enjoy sitting with me when I wrote my books. She enjoyed play far more than the presence of The Holy Spirit in The Secret Place. A minister friend explained gently with me, "Mike, she simply has not been captivated by what has captivated you." It is not enough for your mate to be captivated by you; *they must be stirred by the same thing that stirs you.*

I often speak at women's conferences. I always emphasize that you cannot know a man by studying *him.* You know a man by *studying his focus.*

5. Think Twice If You Have Lost Your Desire To Impress Them. I watched a wife wave good-bye to her husband one morning. She was at the front door waving. Missing buttons, a torn pocket and breakfast stains on her gown, and her hair up in rollers—she was everything a man wants to *forget.* I understood easily why he was so excited about driving off to work...where someone would greet him at the door with a bright smile, pressed clothes and perfume to *impress* him.

You are a walking message system to those you love. Would you fly on a plane with seats broken, egg on the tie of the pilot, missing buttons and torn seats? Of course not. You would think, "That's *visible* damage. What else has not been corrected in the engine?"

Something is wrong when you no longer desire to present your best to your Mate.

I was so impressed one day when I saw a friend's wife set the table with the most expensive silverware and fine china for her husband. She explained to me, "The most special person in my life is my husband. I would never save my beautiful silverware for an occasional visitor when my husband is the king of this house."

6. Think Twice If They Never Ask Quality Questions Concerning Your Greatest Dreams And Goals. Questions reveal desire. Questions reveal humility.

7. Think Twice If They Ignore Worthy Counsel From Qualified Mentors In Their Life. Who are their *heroes?* You become like those you admire. You adapt the habits of those you envy. Who is their dominant *Mentor?* At whose feet do they sit consistently? A Mentor is a prophecy of a Protegé. If they rebel against the counsel of their pastor, they are living undisciplined, uncovered and unadvised. Tragedy is scheduled.

8. Think Twice If They Have Not Yet Impressed Their Pastor. I was attracted to a lady and inquired about her to the pastor and his wife. They exchanged glances and said quietly,

"She has come a long way." I understand *preacher talk*. That simply said, she is a long way from where she should really be.

9. Think Twice If You Do Not See Continuous Improvement In The Relationship. Improvement is revealed by the *decrease of conflict*. Conflict occurs through opposite goals, philosophies or beliefs. Bonding should increase unity and bring a decrease in contention and strife.

Strife Is The Evidence Of Opposite Belief Systems.

10. Think Twice If They Show Little Pain Or Remorse Concerning Their Past Mistakes And Sins. Those who are truly repentant truly hurt. Repentant people are not arrogant. Repentant people do not blame others for their decisions. Memories of mistakes *should* produce sorrow and heartache. When regret is not expressed, the offense usually occurs again. Some people never repent for past mistakes. Why? They have not tasted the painful consequences of their rebellion. They do not possess a true fear of God. They believe they are beyond judgment. It is futile to pursue a relationship with someone who does not possess an obvious fear of God.

Uncorrected Conduct Becomes Repeated Conduct. The *fear of God* keeps a mate faithful. Beauty will not. One lady explained to me, "I will keep myself so beautiful, he will not even look at another woman." How foolish! *Your* beauty does not make *another* woman ugly.

Beauty cannot guarantee faithfulness.

The fear of God keeps us faithful.

Some of the best articles written are in women's magazines. However, it saddens me deeply to watch some Mentors of women teach the art of manipulation, intimidation and deception to deceive the men they are pursuing. *You will never respect anyone you are capable of deceiving.*

11. Think Twice If They Enjoy The Climate And Atmosphere Of Rebels. I met a very striking lady who was a brilliant conversationalist. Quite impressive. Classy. Elegant. Knowledgeable. Something did not seem quite right, but I ignored it. One day she exclaimed excitedly, "Oh, I just love working with homosexuals. They are just so enjoyable. I would rather work around homosexuals than anyone." She was unoffended by sin.

Obviously, God loves every one of us regardless of our sin. However, anything that *grieves* the heart of God *should* grieve us.

Anything that angers *God* should anger *you.*

Anything that saddens *God* should sadden *you.*

If you insist on dating someone comfortable with rebellious, stubborn, arrogant, God-despising people...you will be heartbroken.

An actress became a personal friend. Excellent conversationalist. Appeared to love God with all of her heart. Continuously I heard, "My best friend this...my best friend...we have been best friends for a million years." Then, I found out that her best friend has been living with a man for fourteen years. Her best friend sneers at the law of God, belittles preachers and thinks that holy living is a joke. Yet, this was her *best* friend! This was her *confidante!* Yet, she was completely comfortable in the presence of someone living in defiance of God. A godly relationship for us was impossible.

12. Think Twice If The Atmosphere Of Unbelievers Excites Them. I once heard the wife of a preacher say, "I just love to go to the shows in Las Vegas. I enjoy Tom Jones and the atmosphere so much! He excites me!" Was I shocked over their divorce later? Of course not. The atmosphere of the ungodly excited her flesh and she *fed* it.

I love the presence of God. I crave His Voice. I am ecstatic over His Word. My favorite atmosphere is not a smoke-filled, curse-saturated, filthy-joking, beer-drinking crowd. My favorite atmosphere is the House of God with hands uplifted, loving, praising and worshipping the One who created me.

You have no future with someone who insists on fueling their passion in the atmosphere of the ungodly.

13. Think Twice If They Have An Obsession To Attract The Attention Of The Opposite Sex. Some women are unhappy unless every man in the room gravitates around her as the "center of attention." I have known men who cannot pass by a mirror without sitting down for a while and staring, mesmerized by their perceived beauty.

14. Think Twice If Breaking The Law Is Humorous And Exciting To Them. When I see a radar detector on the dash of a car, I recognize that I am in the presence of someone who despises restraint, sneers at the law and wants the world to know it.

15. Think Twice If They Show Little Respect For The Agenda And Schedule Of Others. I dated a lady for a long time. One night, I waited 45 minutes in the restaurant for her. She finally showed up and explained, "Well, I met some friends that I have not seen in a long time and I just simply forgot the time. Sorry!"

I replied, "I understand. I have been waiting 45 minutes. I regret that the presence of others made you forget me. I am sure God has someone else exciting for your future." It was over.

Your respect for the schedule of others reveals much about you.

16. Think Twice When It Is Obvious That You Will Never Become Their Focus And Assignment. They may enjoy you, laugh with you and even like you. They may even be truly trustworthy as a confidante. But, a Mate is a different matter. When God brings you a Mate, that person becomes your Assignment. The wife of a young preacher was obviously agitated and frustrated. As we drove home from a crusade late one night, she looked at me with great exasperation and said, "I must find out what my Assignment is!"

I replied gently, "He is there *beside* you. God calls him your husband. He is your Assignment. You are his Assignment."

Sadly, I saw continued frustration. Many

marriages of ministers are fragmented today. Good men and women of God are often in miserable marriages. Publicly, their life looks glamorous and exciting. Many are even famous and well known. But, they despise their marriage because they have ceased to view *the other* as their true Assignment.

17. Think Twice When They Embrace An Accusation Against You Before They Have Heard Your Side Of The Matter. Loyalties will be identified and exposed eventually. The weakness of a very important relationship was exposed to me. Late one night, my telephone rang. The young lady tore into me like a hurricane. Not once did she ask me if the details of a situation were *accurate*. She never assumed that those around her might be lying or misinformed. It was absurd. What did I realize? *Truth* was not her focus. My opinion was unimportant. It was a heartbreaking revelation, but I realized that others could lie about me and my explanation would never be valued nor believed.

18. Think Twice If They Have Not Exited Previous Relationships Peaceably. Many thrive on strife. They will destroy anything they cannot own or control. Peace bores them. Silence nauseates them. Warfare is their fuel. They will speak any words necessary to find the boundary lines and limitations around them. It will be impossible to have an enjoyable marriage with them.

19. Think Twice If Their Parents Have Contempt For You Or Your Assignment In Life. The bloodline is more powerful than anyone can imagine. It is a spiritual thing. It is a spirit connection. God arranged it Himself. So, you may marry a rebel who even despises his parents...but when crisis comes, he will reach back to the bloodline for affirmation. If you marry someone whose parents look condescendingly upon you because of your lack of education, social class or finances, remember that they will be the *third party* always speaking into the heart of your mate.

20. Think Twice If They Refuse To Sit Consistently Under The Mentorship Of A Spiritual Leader. Changes will not occur without worthy Mentors or uncommon pain. Unwillingness to sit under the Mentorship of a proven man of God is a devastating revelation of potential failure.

21. Think Twice If Pebble Problems Unleash Mountains Of Anger In Them. I will never forget it as long as I live. While sitting with several friends in a beautiful restaurant, the waiter forgot to bring lime for the water glass of the lady I was dating. She was furious. In fact, not only did she look angry at the waiter, but she decided that his incompetence would become *the focus* of the evening conversation. She could not differentiate between things that were important and things that were trivial.

22. Think Twice If They Refuse To Find A Job. It is a *sin* not to work. I would never allow my daughter to marry a man unwilling to *earn* his living. Money is a reward for solving problems. If you never have any money, you are probably refusing to solve the problems nearest you, or for someone you should. You often hear of a multi-millionaire marrying a waitress he met in a small cafe. Why? He observed her work habits. At three o'clock a.m., she was there bringing pancakes and eggs to truck drivers...with a smile on her face. It was one of the secrets of Solomon. He only hired happy people. It is important to marry someone happy *before* you enter their life.

Paul warned, "This we commanded you, that if any would not work, neither should he eat. For we hear that there are some which walk among you disorderly, working not at all, but are busybodies...And if any man obey not our word by this epistle, note that man, and *have no company with him,* that he may be ashamed," (2 Thessalonians 3:10-11, 14).

Productive women excite productive men. It attracted Boaz to Ruth.

23. Think Twice If Their Own Dreams Are Not Big Enough To Motivate Them. If they can sleep in all day, watch television all night and refuse to produce anything significant with their life...you better think twice before pouring your life into them. Every person should have a dream big enough to get him out of bed every morning or keep him up at night!

24. Think Twice If They Are Uncomfortable In The Presence Of God. As I told one of my sisters, you can date a man who is handsome, has developed muscles and throws you a rose to watch you dive—but if he hates the presence of God, there is no hope of greatness ever being birthed within him. The man you see will never be more than what he is today. Every preacher will become his rival. He will become intimidated by your church attendance. When you come home late after a Wednesday night service, he will accuse you of meeting somebody "on the side." Unsaved men are often intimidated by believing men because they know in their heart that a man who walks with God has something they lack.

25. Think Twice If They Feel Inferior To You. True, everyone is superior to others in some way. But, it is important that those who walk beside you feel confident, qualified and called of God to be your Mate.

26. Think Twice If They Do Not Long To Understand And Pleasure You. Uncommon love longs to pleasure another. Uncommon love seeks every opportunity to communicate itself. What do you enjoy? What books do you love to read? Where do you want to go for vacation? What is your favorite flower? Your Mate should long to know.

27. Think Twice If Continuous Strife Exists Between Them And Their Parents. Honoring our parents was the first commandment with a promise. Those who celebrate the authority over their life ultimately succeed.

28. Think Twice If They Treat The Favor Of Others With Ingratitude. Countless times, I have paid for meals at restaurants and never received a single thanks for it. I dated a lady for many months without receiving a thank you for anything I purchased or did for her during that year. Her explanation, "I simply wasn't taught to say the word 'Thanks.' I will show it in other ways." Absurd.

29. Think Twice If They Do Not Have A Hunger To Know The Voice Of God. Obedience is the secret of every successful person. The Bible is His Voice. If a man or woman disdains *The Voice* of Truth and Wisdom—they will birth a parade of tragedies and catastrophes.

Their *decisions* will create losses.

Their *weaknesses* will flourish.

Unlawful desires will rage like an inferno.

Such a marriage is an invitation to spiritual suicide.

30. Think Twice If You Are Not Excited About Introducing Them To Those You Love. When you are truly in love, that's all you want to talk about. Are you ashamed? Why? Be truthful with yourself.

31. Think Twice If They Show Little Respect For The Battles You Have Won Throughout Your Lifetime. Have you mastered prejudice, fears or poverty? When someone loves you, they admire your achievements.

32. Think Twice If Conversation With Them Has Become Burdensome. I have been with some who left me frazzled, exhausted and I did not know why.

Right people *energize* you.

Wrong people *exhaust* you.

True love will *energize*.

33. Think Twice If They Make The Major Decisions Of Their Life Without Pursuing Your Feedback. I was stunned one night when a lady I had dated for some time suddenly said, "I quit my job last week. I'm going to Bible School tomorrow." She had been considering leaving her career for nine months and going to a Bible School.

She never told me. It was obvious—my feedback was unimportant.

34. Think Twice If Your Time Spent With Them Always Ends With Personal Guilt Or Disappointment. Withdraw from any relationship if guilt, fear or a sense of entrapment emerges.

35. Think Twice If People Of Excellence Do Not Surround Them. Study the kinds of people that your potential mate finds enjoyable. That is a clue to their life and your future with them.

36. Think Twice If They Are Unwilling To Follow Your Personal Advice And Counsel. A godly wife is The Prophetess in the bosom of her husband. A husband should be a Well of Wisdom for his wife.

37. Think Twice If You Do Not Admire And Respect The Mentor At Whose Feet They Sit. Their Mentor is feeding either a strength or a weakness. If you oppose their Mentor, a happy marriage is impossible.

38. Think Twice If You Only Enjoy Them During Your Moments Of Weakness Instead Of Your Moments Of Strength. One woman explained to me, "I don't really want to be with him. I feel very vulnerable around him, but, I am often lonely. So, *when I get so lonely* I can't stand it—I accept his invitation for a date." Some relationships exist because of mutual *weakness,* rather than mutual *goals.*

39. Think Twice If They Continuously Give You Counsel Contrary To The Word Of

God. The Word of God is Truth. It will withstand any test. It destroys wrong desires within you. It unleashes your faith. It produces hope. It purifies your mind. It is the Master Key to all success on earth. *Your reaction to The Word of God determines God's reaction to your own children* (Hosea 4:6). God will become their enemy if they continue to defy His Word. It would be tragic to bond with someone God may ultimately destroy.

40. Think Twice If Their Presence Does Not Motivate You To A Higher Level Of Excellence. You already possess weaknesses. You do not require anyone to *feed* them. Anyone can pull you *down*. That is why God gives you a Mate to lift you *up*.

41. Think Twice If You Cannot Trust Them With The Knowledge Of Your Greatest Weakness. Each of us contain weaknesses that embarrass us. We despise them. It may be anger, fear or lust. Your Mate is there to strengthen you, not weaken you. If you believe it is necessary to *hide* your weakness instead of share it, you may have the wrong Mate.

42. Think Twice If You Cannot Trust Them With Your Finances. This narrows down the field considerably, doesn't it! Do not bond your life with someone too immature to handle the importance of financial responsibility. One young man explained to me, "I do not want my fiancée to know anything about my money or she will spend it. As soon as she discovers I have some extra money, she persuades me to run up my credit cards."

43. Think Twice If You Cannot Trust Them With Your Most Painful Memories. Every person is running from a painful memory. Multi-millionaires often share that their days of poverty have motivated them. Their painful memories have driven them to uncommon achievement. Some explain a father who beat them mercilessly. It left them marked forever. *Memories* are keys to understanding another.

44. Think Twice If You Cannot Trust Them With Your Greatest Fears Or Secrets. Fear often limits us. It should motivate us...to change. It may be the fear of flying, or the dark. It may be a fear of dying with disease. Whatever it is—think twice if the love is not strong enough to destroy fear. "Perfect love casteth out fear," (1 John 4:18).

45. Think Twice If You Cannot Trust Them Around Your Closest Friends. Flirtation is deadly. The death of many marriages begins with flirtation. It is not harmless. Ever.

46. Think Twice If You Cannot Trust Them In Your Absence. Jealously is a cruel dictator and tyrant. It is often unfounded and produced by a painful memory of disloyalty or betrayal. Yet, I have seen many marriages unravel because of a deep sense of distrust. Note the signals.

47. Think Twice If You Cannot Trust Them To Pursue God Without Your Constant Encouragement. Several years ago, I met an exciting woman. She was one of the most articulate, vibrant and lovable humans I had ever known. She is still a friend of mine today. I tried hard to push the relationship through, to engagement and marriage. But, it was this key that opened my understanding. She only attended church because of my persistence, nagging and begging. She really did not know God at all. Nor did she truly desire God. Without the authority of God in her life, any hope of a happy marriage with her was a mere fantasy.

Bring your potential Mate into God's presence with you. Talk to God *together*. Truth will emerge in His presence that cannot emerge anywhere else. *Interrogation will never produce what His presence will.*

Invest the Seed of Time.

Watch it grow.

Time will expose what a thousand investigators could never produce.

Define your present relationships honestly and clearly. If you persist in an unwholesome relationship, painful consequences will teach you.

Never lean to your own understanding. Lean to the heart of God. Ask The Holy Spirit what He sees in those near you. He always will reveal truth to the seeker.

Recognition Of The Mate God Approves For You Will Bring Years Of Joy, Enthusiasm And Fulfillment.

RECOMMENDED BOOKS AND TAPES ON THIS TOPIC

B-14   Seeds of Wisdom on Relationships (32 pages/$3)
B-49   The Proverbs 31 Woman (70 pages/$7)
B-55   20 Keys to a Happier Marriage (48 pages/$7)
B-57   Thirty-One Secrets of An Unforgettable Woman (140 pages/$9)
B-83   The Gift of Wisdom for Wives (32 pages/$10)
B-84   The Gift of Wisdom for Husbands (32 pages/$10)
B-88   The Gift of Wisdom for Brides (32 pages/$10)
B-89   The Gift of Wisdom for Grooms (32 pages/$10)
TS-05   Life As A Christian Single (6 tapes/$30)
TS-16   The Double Diamond Principle in Successful Relationships (6 tapes/$30)
TS-53   Thirty-One Secrets of An Unforgettable Woman (6 tapes/$30)

**"If ye be willing and obedient, ye shall
eat the good of the land."
Isaiah 1:19**

～ 7 ～

RECOGNITION OF A MOMENT OF UNCOMMON FAITH

------➤·◆·❮------

Faith Moves Mountains.

The Master Key to supernatural miracles is the Weapon of Faith. Your mouth is the Tool that unleashes the silent belief lying within you—that confidence in God called *Faith.*

Uncommon Miracles Require Uncommon Faith. God has an obsession to be believed. He withholds from anyone who *doubts* His Word (Isaiah 1:19). He always rewards those who *believe* His Word (Deuteronomy 28:1-14).

In my book, *31 Reasons People Do Not Receive Their Financial Harvest,* I wrote the following:

Tears alone do not *move* God.

Desperation does not *intimidate* God.

Manipulation does not *control* God.

Education does not *influence* God.

Faith is the only voice God *respects.*

Faith is the only method that *impresses* God to activate miracles. You *must* ask in faith.

Faith Comes When You Hear God Talk. "So

then faith cometh by hearing, and hearing by the Word of God," (Romans 10:17).

The two most important qualities that I have learned about God are:

▶ His only *pain* is to be *doubted*.

▶ His only *pleasure* is to be *believed*.

God continuously arranges scenarios that require your confidence in Him.

Nothing good in your life happens until you *use* your faith.

Faith is the Weapon God provides to produce your miracles.

Without Faith, God Cannot Be Pleasured By You. "Without faith it is impossible to please Him: for he that cometh to God must believe that He is, and that He is a rewarder of them that diligently seek Him," (Hebrews 11:6).

Faith Shuts Down When An Option Is Being Considered. "A double minded man is unstable in all his ways," (James 1:8).

At some moment in your life, God's going to give you a dream so big...it will require every ounce of faith in your system.

The Most Dangerous Day In Your Life Is The Day You Do Not Have A Dream Big Enough To Require Uncommon Faith.

Faith Is *Confidence In God.*

Faith Requires An *Instruction.*

Faith Is Activated By *Needs And Desires.* When you do not have a great need in your life, it is a dangerous season.

You will be tempted to live a life without faith. When you attempt it, you will fail miserably.

God's only moments of pleasure are the moments you are using your faith.

Unused Faith Is A Tragedy.

The moment will come when God will show you a picture of a future so big that your present looks tiny and insignificant. At that moment, He gives you a photograph of your future to stir your faith...which brings Him pleasure.

Fear Is The Enemy Of Faith. Each day of fear will produce 365 days of tears and heartache. The Israelites' entry into Canaan was intriguing. Twelve spies entered Canaan. Ten came back with doubt and unbelief. Because of their doubt, God turned their 40 days of spying and doubt into 40 years of pain. *Each day of doubt was multiplied 365 days for their tears and heartache.*

You cannot afford the consequences of a day of doubt in your life.

Doubt Produces Tragedies Like Faith Produces Miracles.

► Your Greatest *Enemy* Is The Person Who Feeds Your *Doubt.*

► Your Greatest *Friend* Is The One That Breathes Life Into Your *Faith.*

Faith Is Confidence In The Greatness Of God, Not Your Personal Greatness.

When God Loves You Enough To Assign Someone To Unlock Your Faith, You Must Recognize It As A Moment Of Uncommon Faith That Produces Your Miracle.

Faith Will Always Require A Specific Instruction. Not three. "This *one* thing I do" was the cry of the great man of God. David cried out, "My heart is fixed," (Psalm 57:7).

Your Faith Is Deciding The Flow Of Miracles That Are Coming Toward You. No faith. No miracles.

One of my greatest Moments of Uncommon Faith is shared in my book, *31 Reasons People Do Not Receive Their Financial Harvest.* I want to quote from page 158:

Several years ago, I was preaching for Rod Parsley, a friend of mine, in Columbus, Ohio. At the end of the service, The Holy Spirit spoke to me to receive an offering for the pastor instead of my own ministry. Well, I desperately needed a miracle. I needed finances badly for a special project I was facing. So, any Seed I planted would be a Crisis Seed. (Remember that a Crisis Seed increases in its influence with God.) *It is possible that a small Seed sown during a crisis produces a greater Harvest than a generous Seed during good times.*

So, I agreed to give the offering in its entirety to the pastor. Then The Holy Spirit made an unusual suggestion. I really did not feel that it was a command but rather an *invitation to an investment.* I had just received a royalty check for $8,500. (Actually, it was everything that I had to my name.) I do not recall any money in my savings account other than this check I had in my briefcase.

"How would you like to *explore and experiment* with what I could do with your $8,500?" The Holy Spirit spoke.

It brought a moment of torment and torture. Then, I just quietly spoke in my spirit back to Him, "That's all right. I really appreciate this wonderful $8,500. It is *enough* Harvest for me."

He spoke the second time. Oh, how thankful

I am for the second chances He gives to us to try again, *reach* again and *plant* again.

"How would you like to *explore and experiment* with what I could do with your $8,500?"

Something in me took a careful evaluation.

What could I really do with $8,500? It certainly was not enough to pay my house off. What could I do? Buy a small car, or put a down payment on a rent house, or fly to Europe and vacation for a month?

I decided to believe His Word.

That decision changed my lifetime income forever. Six weeks later, God gave me an idea that brought me hundreds of thousands of dollars in return. In fact, every 90 days I receive a royalty check for that idea.

My one-time Seed of $8,500 created a Lifetime Income for me. (See Chapter 9, "Recognition Of A God-Inspired Idea.")

You see, I recognize now that God was giving me a *Moment of Uncommon Faith*...to sow everything I had to my name.

It has produced an incredible amount of financial prosperity in my lifetime.

Seize every moment of Uncommon Faith. Do not let go of it. You are standing at the Golden Gate of Miraculous Increase.

Uncommon Faith Always Produces Uncommon Miracles.

Nobody was around me to tell me that I would get a *lifetime blessing* for it. But, it was my *Moment* —my *Moment of Uncommon Faith.*

I am so stirred as I write to you tonight to focus my faith with you. Even now, while you are reading these words, something is jumping up and down within you. *This could be your own Moment of Uncommon Faith.* I will pray now and ask God to unleash a Moment of Uncommon Faith for you.

God may speak to you to plant a Lifetime Seed for a Lifetime Blessing...like He did to me. At first, your Seed of $8,500 may seem ridiculous or impossible. But, think for a moment. Is that the only amount of money you will ever need for the rest of your life? Of course not. Would $8,500 pay your house off today? Probably not. So, that $8,500 is not enough...to meet your need. So, it is obviously not your Harvest God has planned for you. It must be a *Seed.*

As I pray for you, God may give you faith to plant a Seed of $1,000 or $200. Whatever it is, move swiftly. Do not wait a moment longer.

Plant your Seed.

Get it into the soil.

Wrap *expectation* around it.

Move *swiftly* when The Holy Spirit gives you a Moment of Uncommon Faith.

"Father, while speaking these words to the reader today, I feel a stirring in my heart. A powerful stirring. A very unusual anointing moving through my spirit. Now Father, you used *twelve* tribes as a trophy of Your power and what You could do on the earth. Jesus used *twelve* disciples to change the world forever. Even the New Jerusalem has *twelve* gates...as a photograph of Your authority. I ask You for *twelve Uncommon Harvests for Twelve Friends who are reading this book at this moment.* I ask You to move swiftly on those twelve even *now.* I speak Uncommon Faith to them *now.* I wrap my faith around their Seed of

$8,500 or $1,000 or *whatever amount You are speaking into their heart.*

This is their *moment.*

This is their *day.*

This is their Golden Gate to Tomorrow.

This is the moment they have waited a lifetime for—in the Name of Jesus I release their faith *now.*

I take authority over every spirit of poverty, lack and disease that has entered their life.

I command doubt to dissolve and to dissipate. I release a wave of Your presence, Your anointing and uncommon faith into their heart *now.*

In the Name of Jesus, I decree this to be the *Moment of Uncommon Faith* for my friend and partner today. I enter into Agreement and I am not coming out of the Agreement...for the one thousandfold return to The Seed that they sow now...this very day according to Deuteronomy 1:11.

We *obey* You. We move *swiftly.* We will *not* rebel. We release what is in our hand *as a Seed*...to unlock The Harvest You hold in Your hand today. In Jesus' Name. It is done. Amen."

I have written over 200 books, yet have never felt the peculiar and rich anointing on my spirit *like I do now.* In the Name of Jesus, I agree that The Uncommon Seed you sow today will create The Uncommon Harvest you have always dreamed about.

It is done. In Jesus' Name. Now!"

If you are one of the twelve—write me a personal note today. Please write on the left hand side outside the envelope these words: "Moment of Uncommon Faith."

Something incredible is bursting on the horizon of your life.

You know it, too.

Recognition Of A Moment Of Uncommon Faith Could Create Lifetime Blessings For You.

RECOMMENDED BOOKS AND TAPES ON THIS TOPIC

B-47 The Covenant of Fifty-Eight Blessings (82 pages/$8)

B-82 31 Reasons People Do Not Receive Their Financial Harvest (252 pages/$12)

B-104 7 Keys to 1000 Times More (128 pages/$10)

TS-02 The Grasshopper Complex (6 tapes/$30)

TS-08 The Strategy of Hourly Obedience (6 tapes/$30)

TS-21 The Double Diamond Principle in Millionaire Mentality (6 tapes/$30)

TS-30 7 Keys to 1000 Times More (6 tapes/$30)

TS-38 31 Reasons People Do Not Receive Their Financial Harvest (6 tapes/$30)

≈ 8 ≈

RECOGNITION OF YOUR DOMINANT SOURCE OF FAVOR

Uncommon Favor Births Uncommon Success.

Uncommon Favor moved Joseph from the prison to the palace of Pharaoh *in one day.* Nothing is more glorious or more miraculous. Nothing else can create ecstasy like a single experience of Uncommon Favor.

Favor is the secret, hidden and unspoken dream of every human living today. We strive for it, pray for it and even beg for it.

Favor can turn tragedy into triumph...*within moments.*

28 Facts You Should Know About Favor

1. Uncommon Favor Is When God Causes Someone To Desire To Become A Problem Solver In Your Life. It may be a relative, your boss or a stranger. According to the Scriptures, God is the catalyst for linking you to the Golden Connection with someone who blesses you.

2. Uncommon Favor Is A Gift From God That Can Stop If It Is Not Recognized And Celebrated. God does not owe you. Others are not obligated to you. *Men* cannot stop it. "He that openeth, and no man shutteth," (Revelation 3:7).

3. Uncommon Favor Is Only Guaranteed To Those Who Qualify Through Acts Of Obedience. "If thou shalt hearken diligently unto the voice of the Lord thy God...all these blessings shall come on thee, and overtake thee," (Deuteronomy 28:1-2).

4. Uncommon Success Will Require Uncommon Favor From Someone. You cannot work hard enough to get everything you deserve. You cannot work long enough to be debt-free. It will require Uncommon Favor to take giant steps into an Uncommon Dream. "The Lord thy God shall bless thee in all thine increase, and in all the works of thine hands," (Deuteronomy 16:15).

5. Uncommon Favor Is An Attitude Of Goodness Toward You, Not An Exchange Or Payment For Something You Have Done. The world uses "favors" as a substitute for Favor.

A congressman may say to a lobbyist, "I will pass this bill through if you will give me $25,000 for another project." That is an *exchange*. It is a *transaction*. You intimidate and obligate others...through *favors,* not *Favor.* That is the satanic *substitution* for the divine plan of *Favor.*

You will always resent anyone you owe. Satan has always attempted to imitate God. He envies the success of God, the strength of God, and the love that God has generated toward Himself. So, he emulates God. Favor is the *Divine* way, not the substitute.

6. Uncommon Favor Is An Exception To The Rule, Not A Normality. Millions struggle without seeing significant progress. "Except the Lord build the house, they labour in vain that build it," (Psalm 127:1).

7. Uncommon Favor Must Begin As A Seed From You Before It Returns As A Harvest To You. "Be not deceived; God is not mocked: for whatsoever a man soweth, that shall he also reap," (Galatians 6:7).

8. When You Sow Seeds Of Favor Consistently, You Will Reap The Harvest Of Favor Consistently. Erratic Seeds produce erratic Harvests. Seeds of Love, Patience and Forgiveness will begin to grow in your own life.

9. The Seed Of Uncommon Favor Can Grow Over A Period Of Time. Jesus grew in favor with God and man (Luke 2:52).

10. Uncommon Favor Can Make You Wealthy In A Single Day. Ruth experienced this. "So Boaz took Ruth, and she was his wife," (Ruth 4:13). The wealth of Abraham was transferred to Rebekah through Isaac...in a single day.

11. Uncommon Favor Can Silence A Lifetime Enemy Forever. Haman was hung after the king showed Esther and Mordecai Uncommon Favor.

12. Uncommon Favor Can Make You A Household Name In 24 Hours. The king chose Esther to be his queen and a nobody became a somebody...in a single day (Esther 2:16).

13. Uncommon Favor Can Double Your Financial Worth In The Midst Of Your Worst

Tragedy. It happened to Job. "The Lord gave Job twice as much as he had before...So the Lord blessed the latter end of Job more than his beginning," (Job 42:10, 12).

14. Uncommon Favor Can Accelerate The Timetable Of Your Assignment And Destiny. Joseph became Prime Minister within 24 hours...even after false accusations.

15. One Day Of Favor Is Worth A Lifetime Of Labor. Ruth was a peasant woman. She worked hard for her living. She toiled, she sweated and remained poor. But, in a single day, Boaz accepted her as his wife.

16. Uncommon Favor Comes When Uncommon Intercessors Pray For You. Peter experienced this. He was in prison. But, the church prayed. God became involved. The doors of the prison were opened. Peter was released (Acts 12:5).

17. Uncommon Favor Always Begins When You Solve An Uncommon Problem For Someone. Joseph interpreted the dream for the butler. Two years later, his gift made room for him in the palace of Pharaoh (read Genesis 41:42-44).

18. Currents Of Favor Always Flow When You Solve The Problem Nearest You. Many who experience profound waves of Favor have found them suddenly stopped. Their progress is paralyzed. Tragedies break across their life. That is why it is important that you understand this Law of Recognition—recognizing the Dominant Source of Favor God has chosen to bless your life.

19. Uncommon Favor Will Usually Come Through Someone Observing You Who Is Capable Of Greatly Blessing You. Your parents.

Your boss. Your neighbors. Someone you do not even yet know.

20. Uncommon Favor Is Not An Accident, But A Deliberate Design By God To Reward You For Acts Of Obedience Invisible To Others. "If ye be willing and obedient, ye shall eat the good of the land," (Isaiah 1:19).

21. Uncommon Favor Will Stop When You Deliberately Ignore An Instruction From God. Saul ignored the instructions of Samuel to destroy King Agag, and all the Amalekites. Favor stopped. Saul was removed from kingship and David became the king (1 Samuel 15:9-11, 26).

22. The Flow Of Uncommon Favor Is Often Paralyzed Through The Development Of Arrogance And Self-Sufficiency. When Nebuchadnezzar sneered at the authority of God because of his uncommon success, God permitted him to live like a beast in the field...until his humility returned (Daniel 5:20-21).

23. Uncommon Favor Can Stop A Tragedy Instantly In Your Life. It moved Joseph from the prison to Pharaoh's palace in a single day (Genesis 41:39-40). Esther had Favor with the king and saved an entire nation.

24. The River Of Uncommon Favor Will Dry Up When God Observes Greed. "Will a man rob God? Yet ye have robbed Me. But ye say, Wherein have we robbed Thee? In tithes and offerings. Ye are cursed with a curse: for ye have robbed Me, even this whole nation," (Malachi 3:8-9). It is a tragedy, an absurdity and futility to try to breathe Favor into a family or a man whom God has chosen to curse *because of their greed*.

Who has God used the most during your

lifetime to bring provision, encouragement or protection to you?

They are your Dominant Source of Favor.

The first commandment with a promise was to honor your parents. God promised that it would go well with you all the days of your life.

Think for a moment. Your parents paid your bills, fed you, clothed you, sheltered you, educated and trained you, endured your immaturity, tolerated your stumbling and learning days...yet are usually the last to receive your respect, your gifts and your spoken evidences of love.

It is common for a young man to spend more on his new girlfriend within 90 days than he has his mother and father in the last 10 years of his life.

Anything Unrecognized Becomes Unrewarded ...And Will Ultimately Exit Your Life.

Refusing to honor and bless your parents is suicidal. It will destroy you. God guarantees it.

25. Uncommon Favor Is A Seed That Anyone Can Sow Into The Life Of Another. It does not require money, nor genius, nor uncommon skill. It requires love, attentiveness and time.

26. Uncommon Favor Should Be Pursued, Requested And Celebrated. When the servant of Abraham, knelt and asked God to show him Favor, it was appropriate. God is the Source of Favor. He responds to faith and pursuit. Within hours, Rebekah was en route back to Isaac because of the Favor of God.

27. Uncommon Favor Is Often The Only Exit From A Place Of Captivity And Bondage. Joseph knew this. He *requested* Favor from the butler. It eventually came.

28. Uncommon Favor Will Usually Cease When Not Received With Thankfulness. Loss is the quickest cure for unthankfulness.

Stop for a moment.

Identify the *Dominant* Source of Favor in your life.

Have you written a note of appreciation?

Have you sown Favor to your own family?

▶ What you fail to *recognize,* you stop *celebrating.*

▶ What you stop *celebrating,* you stop *rewarding.*

▶ Anything unrewarded will *exit* your life.

Recognition Of Your Dominant Source Of Favor Will Solve A Thousand Problems In Your Life.

RECOMMENDED BOOKS AND TAPES ON THIS TOPIC

B-01   Wisdom for Winning (228 pages/$10)
B-11   Dream Seeds (106 pages/$10)
B-99   Secrets of the Richest Man Who Ever Lived (179 pages/$10)
TS-01 Wisdom for Winning (6 tapes/$30)
TS-11 Dream Seeds (6 tapes/$30)
TS-16 The Double Diamond Principle in Successful Relationships (6 tapes/$30)
TS-25 Secrets of the Richest Man Who Ever Lived (6 tapes/$30)

"I wisdom dwell with prudence and find out knowledge of witty inventions."
Proverbs 8:12

❧ 9 ❧

RECOGNITION OF A GOD-INSPIRED IDEA

━━━●━━━

Ideas Are Golden Gates To Immediate Change.
An idea is a thought, divinely planted by God, that could solve a problem for someone. The Scriptures excite us with the promise of *"witty inventions."* "I wisdom dwell with prudence, and find out knowledge of witty inventions," (Proverbs 8:12).

Methods for creating wealth are guaranteed to the obedient. "But thou shalt remember the Lord thy God: for it is He that giveth thee power to get wealth, that He may establish His covenant which He sware unto thy fathers, as it is this day," (Deuteronomy 8:18).

Many years ago, I planted an incredible Seed in Columbus, Ohio (see Chapter 7). Six weeks later, I was in Houston, Texas, staying at the Hyatt Regency Hotel. It was Tuesday morning, 7:15 a.m., during my second hour of prayer. Suddenly, The Holy Spirit *birthed an idea.* I saw in my spirit a special Bible for mothers. It would contain 2,000 Scriptures to help mothers locate within ten seconds the Scripture appropriate for solving an immediate problem they faced. I called it, *The Mother's Topical Bible.* Then, I saw one in my mind

called *The Father's Topical Bible* especially for
fathers going through difficult places in their life.

Then *The Businessman's Topical Bible,*
exploded in my heart. Then, I saw one especially
designed for teenagers who did not understand
how to find scriptures in the Bible...*The Teenager's
Topical Bible.*

I called a friend in the publishing business.
He was elated.

"Mike, we will print 60,000 leather-bound
editions and see how they sell in the bookstores.
You will receive a small royalty from each one that
sells."

Within months, 1,300 bookstores purchased
every copy of those Bibles. Eventually, paperbacks
were printed. Different translations such as the
Living Bible and New International Version were
made available.

That *idea* unlocked hundreds of thousands of
dollars. Someone told me that almost two million
of those topical Bibles have gone throughout the
earth.

That idea produced blessings for millions.

I recognized it was from *God.* It was *given* to
me. Yes, others have copied it and imitated it. It
was a divinely inspired idea God gave to me.

But, *I had to recognize it.*

Several years ago, while in prayer, The Holy
Spirit gave me another little Bible idea. It is called
the *One-Minute Pocket Bible.* Anyone can carry it
in their shirt pocket. The small *One-Minute Pocket
Bible* has gone throughout America. One of the
greatest television ministries today purchased
thousands for their partners. Every Mother's Day,

pastors give these pocket Bibles and topical Bibles to ladies in their church.

Good ideas are interesting but are not commands.

God ideas are actually God commands. They awaken you in the middle of the night, becoming your obsession.

Oral Roberts once explained that when God promised you more than you *"have room to receive,"* He was speaking of ideas, insights and concepts. He instructed the people to *review* any idea, insight or concept God had given them and then present it to God for blessing.

One man listened with great faith. Years prior, he had had an idea. It was repeatedly rejected. He became demoralized and discouraged with it. He had stored it in boxes in his attic. After hearing Brother Roberts, he decided that the idea was from God. Satan had simply paralyzed his expectations and faith.

He went home, crawled into his attic and brought the boxes back down. Today, he is worth over one hundred million dollars...*because of that idea.*

Are you sitting on a million-dollar idea? Are you chasing pennies...when God gave you a million-dollar concept?

Years ago, I was speaking in Dothan, Alabama. When I finished preaching, I asked the people to give their Seed an Assignment as they planted the Seed in the offering.

"Write on your check where you most need to see your Harvest today," I instructed.

Some months later, I returned to the church.

The pastor was exhilarated.

"I want you to meet this couple. Do you remember asking the people to give their Seed an Assignment? You told them to write on the check where they would like to see God produce their Harvest the most."

He explained that within 90 days from the time they had planted their Seed, an idea that had been ignored and rejected was suddenly accepted by a major grocery chain. Their *first* check for the their first order was for *2.4 million dollars.*

Their idea was worth 2.4 million dollars.

Ross Perot, the famed billionaire, said *"One Good Idea Can Enable A Man To Live Like A King The Rest Of His Life."*

Enter God's presence to receive His *commands.*

Stay in God's presence to receive His *plan.*

God is talking to you.

Are you listening?

8 Facts You Should Know About Ideas

1. An Uncommon Idea Comes Through Observation Of What Is Around You.

2. An Uncommon Idea Will Help People.

3. An Uncommon Idea From God Will Solve Problems For Somebody.

4. An Uncommon Idea Is A Solution That Eliminates Stress, Increases Enthusiasm And Joy.

5. An Uncommon Idea Can Come To You Whether It Is Respected By Those Around You Or Not. Walt Disney was fired from a newspaper because he was "not creative enough."

6. An Uncommon Idea Can Create Uncommon Wealth.

7. An Uncommon Idea Requires Uncommon Attention.

8. An Uncommon Idea Can Create A Lifetime Of Provision.

Recognition Of A God-Inspired Idea That Provides A Lifetime Income For Your Family.

RECOMMENDED BOOKS AND TAPES ON THIS TOPIC:

B-11   Dream Seeds (106 pages/$9)

B-99   Secrets of the Richest Man Who Ever Lived (179 pages/$10)

B-100   The Holy Spirit Handbook, Vol. 1 (153 pages/$10)

B-104   7 Keys to 1000 Times More (128 pages/$10)

TS-11   Dream Seeds (6 tapes/$30)

TS-18   The Double Diamond Principle in Gifts, Goals and Greatness (6 tapes/$30)

TS-25   Secrets of the Richest Man Who Ever Lived (6 tapes/$30)

TS-29   The Holy Spirit Handbook (6 tapes/$30)

"No good thing will He withhold from
them that walk uprightly."
Psalm 84:11

∾ 10 ∾

RECOGNITION OF A GOLDEN OPPORTUNITY

Opportunity Is A Gift From God.

Opportunity is any situation where your favorable qualities and skills, known or unknown, can be recognized, received and ultimately rewarded.

4 Facts You Should Know About Opportunity

1. God Is The God Of Opportunity. Throughout The Word, countless examples remind us that God gives men an opportunity to repent, rebuild and even receive miracles.

2. Opportunities Are Often Overlooked Because Of Immaturity Or Ignorance. One of my closest friends was invited to make a choice years ago: an automobile or a piece of land in Florida. He chose the automobile. Sadly, the land he rejected was connected to the famed Disney World. He lost a fortune because of it. He did not *recognize* the Golden Opportunity for investment.

3. An Opportunity Can Even Be Given To You During A Crisis Season Of Your Life. God spoke to Elijah to leave the brook and go to the widow of Zarephath...to give her an opportunity to use her faith (1 Kings 17).

4. **An Opportunity Is Always Near You, Merely Awaiting Your Recognition Of It.** "No good thing will He withhold from them that walk uprightly," (Psalm 84:11).

You Must Learn To Recognize These 8 Golden Opportunities

1. **Recognition Of An Opportunity For Uncommon Mentorship.** Elisha did and pursued Elijah. Ruth embraced Naomi, refusing to go back to Moab.

2. **Recognition Of An Opportunity For A Miracle Of Healing.** Blind Bartimaeus did. He cried out and received his healing.

3. **Recognition Of An Opportunity To Be Rewarded For Destroying An Enemy.** David did. He conquered Goliath.

4. **Recognition Of An Uncommon Friendship That Can Bring Countless Joy.** Jonathan did. He became known for his loyalty to David.

5. **Recognition Of An Opportunity For Financial Breakthrough.** The widow of Zarephath did. Years ago, I received a telephone call. A friend of mine was involved in a networking organization. He flew out and assisted me. God helped me in a wonderful way. I made thousands of dollars. Yet, others around me never saw the opportunity. They were too busy complaining how hard it was to do.

6. **Recognition Of An Opportunity For Significance.** David did. He killed Goliath.

7. Recognition Of An Opportunity To Erase The Memory Of Every Stigma Of Your Life.

8. Recognition Of An Opportunity For Access To An Uncommon Man Of God. Oral Roberts once related to me that young preachers had spent hours with him without asking a single question about Divine Healing. How tragic!

Recognition Of A Golden Opportunity Can Turn A Dull Life Into Uncommon Success.

RECOMMENDED BOOKS AND TAPES ON THIS TOPIC

B-13   Seeds of Wisdom on Dreams & Goals (32 pages/$3)
B-15   Seeds of Wisdom on Miracles (32 pages/$3)
B-82   31 Reasons People Do Not Receive Their Financial Harvest (252 pages/$12)
TS-08   The Strategy of Hourly Obedience (6 tapes/$30)
TS-38   31 Reasons People Do Not Receive Their Financial Harvest (6 tapes/ $30)

"Let the Lord be magnified, which
hath pleasure in the prosperity of His
servant."
Psalm 35:27

~ 11 ~

RECOGNITION OF A FINANCIAL DELIVERER GOD SENDS INTO YOUR LIFE

Poverty Is Tormenting.

Poverty is a thief. It steals much more than your finances. It steals your dream. It steals your sense of worth. It steals your significance. It steals your ability to bless those around you.

God wants to bless you financially. He is a giver. "Let the Lord be magnified, which hath pleasure in the prosperity of His servant," (Psalm 35:27).

Financial Deliverers are special gifts from a caring Father.

Few true Financial Deliverers exist.

In Seminars, I sometimes offer a $100 bill to anyone who can give me a list of ten names on the face of the earth whose sole and exclusive anointing is for the Financial Deliverance of the body of Christ.

Nobody ever collects.

Many discuss it *briefly.*

But, few make Financial Deliverance their *total focus.*

The anti-prosperity cult has raised its head.

The agitation a Financial Deliverer creates is incredible and remarkable.

Any pastor who focuses on financial deliverance sets in motion a systematic and methodical effort to destroy his credibility in that city.

Arguments are presented.

"Well, Dr. Mike, I just believe we ought to have balance. Some of these preachers focus only on money, money, money."

I replied, "Does it disgust you that your dentist works only on your teeth and refuses to mow your grass? Are you mad at your lawyer because he won't wash your car? Have you quit going to McDonald's because they will not sell you any Chinese food?"

Your eyes do not hear.

Your ears do not talk.

Why do you leave them on your face? Because each has a distinct and separate function.

You want to argue *balance?* Then explain why thousands of preachers preach John 3:16 and ignore Mark 10:28-30? *This* is imbalance.

▶ Forty percent of the bankruptcies involve born-again Christians, according to reports.

▶ Ninety-eight percent of lottery winners are reported to be bankrupt within 24 months after they win a lottery, according to one commentator.

▶ Widows in our local churches often cannot even pay their apartment rent.

▶ Churches are crammed with single mothers unable to even afford daycare for their little child.

Yet, many are angry at the prosperity message.

"Well, God will provide and take care of the people whether we minister on prosperity or not," said one pastor to me.

That logic guarantees that every sinner will be saved...whether he hears about it or not. Every sick body will be healed...whether they hear the faith message on healing or not. Paul wrote, Romans 10:14-15: "...how shall they hear without a preacher? And how shall they preach, except they be sent?"

7 Reasons God Will Schedule A Financial Deliverer Into Your Life

1. God Wants To Provide You Finances That Help You Pay Your Taxes And Obligations. "Render therefore unto Caesar the things which are Caesar's; and unto God the things that are God's," (Matthew 22:21).

2. God Wants You To Have Enough Finances To Give Gifts To Your Children And Those You Love. "If ye then, being evil, know how to give good gifts unto your children, how much more shall your Father which is in Heaven give good things to them that ask Him?" (Matthew 7:11).

3. God Wants You To Have Enough Finances To Help The Poor. "He that hath pity upon the poor lendeth unto the Lord; and that which He hath given will He pay him again," (Proverbs 19:17).

**4. God Wants You To Have Enough

Finances To Send Ministers Throughout The Earth Preaching The Gospel. "And how shall they preach, except they be sent? as it is written, How beautiful are the feet of them that preach the gospel of peace, and bring glad tidings of good things!" (Romans 10:15).

5. God Wants You To Have Enough Finances To Provide What Your Family Needs To Unlock Their Success And Future. "But if any provide not for his own, and specially for those of his own house, he hath denied the faith, and is worse than an infidel," (1 Timothy 5:8).

6. God Wants You To Have Enough Finances To Provide A Generous And Worthy Income For Your Spiritual Leaders And Pastor. "Let the elders that rule well be counted worthy of double honour, especially they who labour in the Word and doctrine. For the scripture saith, Thou shalt not muzzle the ox that treadeth out the corn. And, The labourer is worthy of his reward," (1 Timothy 5:17-18).

Your *needs* matter.

Your *desires* are felt.

7. God Is Pleasured Through Your Personal Prosperity. "Let the Lord be magnified, which hath pleasure in the prosperity of His servant," (Psalm 35:27).

Money does not create *joy*.

Money creates *ability*. With it, you express love, pay bills, solve problems. "Money answereth all things," (Ecclesiates 10:19).

Yet, nothing changes until you use your faith.

That is why the most glorious moment of your financial life is when God births *uncommon faith in the presence of a man of God.* God knows the moment you need a Financial Deliverer in your life.

That is why He sent Elijah to the widow of Zarephath. She was broke, impoverished and on her last meal. Her son was about to die. But, God scheduled a man of God to cross her life...*to unlock her faith.*

Elijah was her Financial Deliverer.

The Washington, D.C. Miracle

Some years ago, in Washington, D.C., The Holy Spirit impressed me to plant a $58 Seed representing the 58 kinds of blessings in The Word of God that I had discovered and categorized. The Holy Spirit instructed me to plant an extra Seed of $58...and write the name of my son, Jason, on the check. He was twelve at the time. His mother and I had experienced a divorce eleven years prior. I had spent and lost over $50,000 in two child custody cases. His mother had married several times. She had only attended one of my services in eleven years. I knew the principle of *giving your Seed an Assignment.* David saw 70,000 people die in 72 hours and stopped the plague by bringing a Seed to God (read 2 Samuel 24).

Within a few weeks, I landed back at the Dallas/Fort Worth Airport. My secretary was standing there with incredible news.

"Jason will be here in one hour at the other airport."

"'What's wrong?" I replied, stunned.

"Nothing. His mother has just decided he can

come spend the rest of his life with you."

Within 90 days, tears streamed down her face as she sat in my little Wisdom Room in my offices. She started sending my ministry $100 a month! Now, that is a true miracle!

It Happened In South Carolina

Later I was in South Carolina. At the close of the service, The Holy Spirit impressed me to relate the story of The Seed of $58 I had planted in Washington, D.C. I have spoken about this hundreds of places around the world. The results have been remarkable.

I told them in South Carolina about the miracle of the $58 Seed.

That afternoon, a man called the pastor and accused me of being a con artist...conning people out of $58!

I jokingly asked the pastor, "Am I that cheap-looking!"

Several years passed. Recently, I was speaking at New Life Bible College in Cleveland, Tennessee. I told the story about this man calling me a con.

A lady stood to her feet and requested a moment to say something. I agreed.

"We just moved here from South Carolina. *My brother* was the one who said that you were a con. I spoke negatively about your ministry for a lot of years and...was convicted in a church here...the Lord told me to submit to your ministry if I was looking for a financial miracle." She told privately that her brother had lost everything and was facing bankruptcy.

Her brother did not recognize a Financial Deliverer God had sent that Sunday morning.

In the same service, a lady pastor from Charlotte, North Carolina, was present. She took out her checkbook and started planting $58 Seeds. Within a few months, an elderly man that she had purchased medicine for, died suddenly. She thought he was impoverished. After his death, she discovered that he was not poor at all. In fact, he left her: 1) a church completely debt-free, 2) two houses debt-free, and 3) 27 acres of ground debt-free. Two years later, the geological report came back and they had found gold on her 27 acres of ground.

Recognition Of A Financial Deliverer Works.

23 Facts About Financial Deliverers

1. A Financial Deliverer May Have An Abrasive Personality That Makes You Uncomfortable.

2. A Financial Deliverer May Appear Over-Confident Because He Has Been Fed Miraculously While Living Alone By The Brook. (See 1 Kings 17.)

3. A Financial Deliverer May Appear To Have Little Interest In Conversation About Your Pain. Elijah did not elaborate and request to see the emaciated body of the widow's son.

4. A Financial Deliverer May Appear Controlling And Authoritative. Elijah told her exactly what to do for him.

5. The Financial Deliverer May Give

You Instructions You Do Not Want To Obey.
Elijah instructed the widow to bring him a meal.

   6. **A Financial Deliverer May Appear To Lack Understanding About A Financial Crisis.** Elijah never even mentioned the dried up brook.

   7. **A Financial Deliverer May Appear To Lack Compassion For The Problems You Are Facing.** Elijah never even showed his tears or pain over her predicament.

   8. **A Financial Deliverer Is Focused On The Law That Provides Your Escape, Not The Painful Memories You Are Replaying.**

   9. **A Financial Deliverer Recognizes That Your Doubt Has Stopped Your Miracle And It Is His Responsibility To Unlock Your Faith.**

   10. **A Financial Deliverer Sees A Different Future Because You Are Obsessed With Your Present.**

   11. **A Financial Deliverer May Never Disclose His Own Secret Pain And Difficulties.** You see, God has brought him through it. He knows the pain. He knows the loss. But, his job is to set you free.

   12. **A Financial Deliverer Confronts Your Greatest Enemy...Doubt.**

   13. **A Financial Deliverer Changes Your Focus.** Elijah painted a portrait of provision.

   14. **A Financial Deliverer Will Speak Words That Unleash Your Faith.** Nothing changes without your faith. Elijah was a Financial Deliverer for the widow of Zarephath. His anointing

broke the spirit of poverty off the widow.

15. A Financial Deliverer Has Often Faced The Same Enemy You Are Facing. Elijah had tasted the pain of a dried up brook. He felt her sense of helplessness, because he had been there.

16. A Financial Deliverer Has Fought The Demon Of Fear And Won. That is why he is qualified to set you free.

17. A Financial Deliverer Talks Expectations While Captives Want To Discuss Their Experiences.

18. A Financial Deliverer Discusses The Future While Captives Want To Discuss The Past.

19. A Financial Deliverer Intimidates Your Enemy, While A Captive Is Intimidated By The Enemy.

20. A Financial Deliverer Has A Different Focus Than The Captives. Captives focus on their *losses.* Deliverers focus on their *victory.* Captives become obsessed with their *pain.* Deliverers are focused on your *future.*

21. A Financial Deliverer Will Focus On Breaking Your Chains, Not Understanding Them. Some will study how they created their crisis. The Financial Deliverer will certainly expose your enemy, but will direct your focus and attention to being free.

22. It Is Your Responsibility To Recognize The Financial Deliverer God Has Assigned To You. He may not *look* like a deliverer. He may not *talk* like a deliverer. He may not *act* like a deliverer. But, he is the Golden Key to your life.

23. When You Embrace The Teaching Of A Financial Deliverer God Has Sent, Your Circumstances Will Change Instantly. "Believe in the Lord your God, so shall ye be established; believe His prophets, so shall ye prosper," (2 Chronicles 20:20).

My Mother Recognized An Anointing

An interesting experience came through my mother. She called me into her little Wisdom Room one day.

"Son, I want to share something personally with you. There is an anointing on your life that I do not understand. I love all my children. All of my children have been blessed of the Lord. But, there seems to be a very unusual anointing on your life. The blessing of the Lord is on you. I have never known anyone in my entire lifetime to receive such blessings of the Lord. I don't really understand it, but I have watched your life. Now, Daddy does not know that I have saved up this money, so don't tell him. You said that you broke the back of poverty with a Seed of $1,000. You have always said that something happens at $1,000 faith that doesn't happen anywhere else. So, here's my special Seed of $1,000."

I sat stunned and quite uncomfortable. This was my precious mother. I knew how limited her personal finances had always been. I immediately said, "Mother, God has been so good to me. I do not need your Seed of $1,000. All of our bills are paid. The ministry is going strong. I will pray for you, though, that God will bless you."

She was adamant and a little bit agitated over it. "No, son. I must plant this Seed. It's very important to me. I want you to pray that God will bless me and let that Anointing for Blessing come on my life also."

Let me digress a moment.

The Boaz Anointing

Everywhere I go, God has been directing me to pray a "Boaz Anointing" on the $1,000 Seed. Here's what is behind it.

Ruth valued Boaz and the blessing on his life. Later, she became the wife of Boaz and everything he had *entered her life as well.*

▶ The Anointing You *Respect* Is The
  Anointing That Moves Toward You.

▶ The Anointing You *Serve* Is The
  Anointing That Multiplies In Your Life.

▶ The Anointing You *Sow Into* Is The
  Anointing That Increases In Your Own
  Life.

So, I have shared publicly how I broke the back of poverty with a Seed of $1,000.

What You Can Walk Away From, You Have Mastered. When you can walk away from an offering that generous you have mastered greed in your life.

Back to my story about mother: I held her faith-filled check of $1,000 in my hand and prayed that God would miraculously start a new blessing in her life.

Within a few days, I stood in a small church

in Pennsylvania. On a Monday morning, as I recall, the pastor and his wife stood with tears in their eyes.

"Dr. Mike, we have never met your mother and father. We would love to. But, the Board felt that we should bless your mother and father." *They handed me $2,000!* One-half was designated for mother and the other half was designated for my father.

Her Seed of $1,000 had already set the blessing in motion...nine days later.

If, like the widow, you are facing a famine, I know beyond a doubt, that the Jehovah Jireh of this universe...has scheduled an Elijah, a Financial Deliverer, into your life.

My question is, *"Can you recognize him?"*

Recognition Of A Financial Deliverer Can Smash The Locks On Your Prison Forever.

RECOMMENDED BOOKS AND TAPES ON THIS TOPIC

B-47   The Covenant of Fifty-Eight Blessings (82 pages/$8)

B-82   31 Reasons People Do Not Receive Their Financial Harvest (252 pages/$12)

B-91   The Leadership Secrets of Jesus (196 pages/$10)

B-99   Secrets of the Richest Man Who Ever Lived (179 pages/$10)

B-104 7 Keys to 1000 Times More (128 pages/$10)

TS-02 The Grasshopper Complex (6 tapes/$30)

TS-21 The Double Diamond Principle in Millionaire Mentality (6 tapes/$30)

TS-25 Secrets of the Richest Man Who Ever Lived (6 tapes/$30)

TS-30 7 Keys to 1000 Times More (6 tapes/$30)

TS-38 31 Reasons People Do Not Receive Their Financial Harvest (6 tapes/$30)

≈ 12 ≈

RECOGNITION OF A MAN OF GOD

You Are A Captive Or A Deliverer.

Men And Women Of God Are *Deliverers.*

They are those who have *recognized* the authority of God and submitted. They have recognized the *plan* of God and cooperated. They have recognized the *consequences of disobeying* their God, and obeyed.

They hate doubt and unbelief.

They fear God.

They keep His commandments.

They are obsessed with doing the will of God on the earth.

Yet, like the Pharisees, millions do not recognize The Man of God assigned to bring change and revolution to their life.

The counsel of pastors is often ignored.

The predictions of prophets are treated lightly.

The world scoffs on late night talk shows at ministers of the gospel.

Scorners do not recognize them.

The rebellious refuse to recognize them.

The ignorant belittle their counsel.

Two classes of people exist on the earth: Deliverers and Captives. Captives are those imprisoned by sin, habits, error, philosophy or anything that prevents them from entering excellence, perfection and a life in The Spirit.

Deliverers think differently than captives.

▶ Captives *discuss* pain.
▶ Deliverers *destroy* pain.

▶ Captives think Deliverers do not care.
▶ Deliverers care enough to fight.

▶ Captives crave *attention*.
▶ Deliverers crave *freedom*.

Deliverers Are Anointed To Set Captives Free. "The Spirit of the Lord God is upon me; because the Lord hath anointed me to preach good tidings unto the meek; He hath sent me to bind up the brokenhearted, to proclaim liberty to the captives, and the opening of the prison to them that are bound," (Isaiah 61:1).

The Anointing Causes Deliverers To Assess The Enemy Accurately. That's why Deliverers hate chains and bondage and want to set Captives free.

I remember when one of my dogs had a thorn embedded in its paw. But, when I tried to help it, it moved away from me yelping. My dog *needed* help, but the pain had become its focus so much that it did not appreciate my desire and ability to help.

That reminds me a lot of hurting people. They are so obsessed with pain, memories and burdens that when a Deliverer arrives, they are often blinded to him.

20 Important Facts About Men And Women Of God

1. True Men Of God Are Necessarily Different Because Their Assignments Are Different. John the Baptist had a different Assignment than the Apostle Paul. Billy Graham has a different Assignment than Benny Hinn. God uses our differences in background, personality and viewpoint to achieve His desired end.

2. Men Of God Do Not Always Understand Each Other. Peter and Paul had their differences. Throughout history, great men have not always been in agreement. Job said, "Great men are not always wise," (Job 32:9).

3. Men And Women Of God Sometimes Experience Failure, Too. Jonah is not the only disobedient man of God in history. Micah is not the only disappointed and discouraged prophet who ever lived. Elijah was not the last prophet who wanted to commit suicide.

The Man of God is a barometer for those to whom he is assigned. He feels their pain. He has tasted disappointment. That increases his effectiveness in relating to others.

4. Men And Women Of God Sometimes Rebel Against Their Assignment. Jonah did (Jonah 1-4).

5. Men And Women Of God Often Exude The Authority Of God That Intimidates Some While Invigorating Others. Stephen's message brought anger to many, and yet deliverance to others.

6. Men And Women Of God Are The Most Gentle Tools God Uses To Deal With People.

The Israelites rebelled against Moses. He taught. He cried. He begged. But, when they ignored the Voice of the Man of God, judgment followed. God opened up the earth and swallowed some. Fire scorched others.

7. Men Of God May Not Be Packaged Like You Anticipated. John the Baptist might not be accepted today, but God was with him.

8. Men Of God Do Not Always Have Comfortable And Enjoyable Personalities. Isaiah and Ezekiel might not be very popular with most Christians today.

9. Men Of God Do Not Always Use The Words Of Academic Excellence And Higher Education. God often uses the heart of the humble over the silken voice of the gifted (read 1 Corinthians 2:1-4).

10. Men Of God Do Not Always Recognize When God Has Spoken To Another Man Of God. They simply must respect the fact that they too are men of God. "Believe in the Lord your God, so shall ye be established; believe His prophets, so shall ye prosper," (2 Chronicles 20:20).

11. Men Of God Are Not Always Adapted Socially. God uses foolish things to confound the wise.

12. The Decisiveness Of Men Of God Is Often Unsettling To The Uncertain. (See John 19:11-12)

13. The Holiness Of Men Of God Agitates The Unholy. (See Acts 7:54-59.)

14. The Courage Of Men Of God Often Enrages The Manipulators. (See Acts 16:17-24.)

15. The Price Paid For Ignoring A Man Of

God Is Often Devastating. Remember Ananias and Sapphira lying to Peter?

16. Ignoring The Man Of God Who Fuels Your Faith Can Create A Lifetime Of Losses. When the Israelites ignored the faith of Moses, Joshua and Caleb, they spent 40 more years of tears, wandering in the wilderness.

17. When You Disrespect Or Disdain A Man Of God, Tragedy May Result. It happened when the children of Israel laughed at the prophet Elisha, calling him an old "bald head."

18. Disrespect Of A Man Of God Will Create A Loss Of Relationship With Him. The Pharisees sneered at Jesus. You never saw Him eating supper with them, either. But, when Zacchaeus, the ungodly tax collector, respected Jesus—Jesus provided him access. Their meal together changed the course of the tax collector's life.

19. The Ungodly Sometimes Recognize A Man Of God Before The Religious Crowd Does. Zacchaeus recognized Jesus while the Pharisees did not. Pharaoh, the leader of Egypt, saw the Spirit of God in Joseph (read Genesis 42).

20. Recognition Of A Man Of God Creates Access To Him. Saul disrespected David. David fled. But Saul's son Jonathan, who recognized the mantle on David, received complete access to him.

8 Hindrances To Recognizing A Man Of God

1. Pride Can Blind You To A Man Of God. The Pharisees were filled with spiritual pride. They did not even recognize Jesus as the Son of God. Yet, a sinful tax collector, Zacchaeus, did *recognize* him. Jesus *responded*.

2. Guilt Can Blind You To A Man Of God. When people feel guilty over their sin, they are intimidated by the presence of a holy man or woman of God. Stephen is an example. When he preached, conviction smote their hearts. They stoned Stephen (Acts 7).

3. Jealousy Often Blinds Us To Men And Women Of God. Nothing is deadlier than envying the way God uses other men and women. King Saul is an example. David was the delight of the Israelites. He was loved by everyone. Saul became jealous. His jealousy blinded him to the greatness and giftings of David. He even attempted to kill David. Yet, Jonathan, his son, *recognized David as a Man of God.*

Jealousy and envy have robbed us of many blessings that God could give to us. Ministers must avoid the trap of *comparison*. When another man of God has thousands attending his services, his responsibility is equal to that kind of reward. None of us realize the pressure and stress that uncommon success creates. We envy how crowds respond to others, and rarely pray for that man of God to be able to endure the hardships it creates.

4. Wrong Voices Of Influence Can Blind You To A Man Of God. When the children of Bethel sneered and belittled Elisha and cried out, "Go up, thou bald head," (2 Kings 2:23)—there is a key here. Obviously, their parents had influenced them. It is dangerous when parents speak contemptuously of men and women of God. I have heard horrifying statements from the mouths of so-called Christian parents, regarding television evangelists. Later, their children continued that same distorted viewpoint.

Assess continually the attitudes of those who are influencing your life. Every Mentor has prejudices. The Uncommon Protegé must detect them and edit them from his own life.

5. Prejudiced Mentors Can Blind You To Worthy Men And Women Of God. If your Spiritual Mentor has had a distasteful experience with a healing ministry, he may prejudice you against healing ministries. If he is offended by prosperity preaching, you could be subconsciously perpetuating that distortion against those who preach uncommon blessing from an uncommon God.

6. Arrogance Can Blind You To A Man Of God. Haman resented Mordecai greatly. When Mordecai refused to bow down to him, Haman purposed to destroy him. It is a horrifying but true story in the book of Esther. Haman, celebrated by the king, had an evil heart. Mordecai knew it. The arrogance of Haman blinded him to the greatness of Mordecai.

7. Your Personal Agenda Can Blind You To A Man Of God. Several years ago, I held a World Wisdom Conference. Nancy Harmon, a dear friend, told me that a minister friend of mine felt led to receive an offering for my ministry. I ignored the request, because I had already received the offering according to the schedule. I did not want to break the rhythm and my plans for the conference. Another minister approached me and repeated what Nancy had said. I explained my schedule and plans were in place already. Finally, the man of God himself approached me, crying.

"I really feel led by The Spirit to receive an offering for your ministry, Mike." He said, through his tears. Reluctantly, I agreed.

Within fifteen minutes, people poured out of their seats to sow Seeds. Over $100,000 in cash and faith promises was committed. I stood to the side quietly. Not one time did I feel God in the whole process. It was shocking to me. As the host of the conference, I felt responsible for hearing The Voice of God over everything that occurred. But He chose to speak to others without confirming it to my own spirit.

I learned something vital that day.

It is important to recognize a Man of God even when you fail to hear The Voice of God personally.

A fascinating illustration is in 1 Kings 17. When the widow received the instruction from the prophet, there is no mention that God confirmed that instruction in her heart. In fact, the opposite occurs. The Bible simply says, "She went and did according to the *saying of Elijah,*" (1 Kings 17:15). Not The Holy Spirit. Not her own inner voice. She *recognized* a man of God and obeyed his instruction explicitly. The miracle came. She never lacked.

8. Familiarity Often Blinds You To Men And Women Of God. Pastors experience the torment of this. Because their people see them in every day situations, their humanity is quickly apparent. Unfortunately, their weaknesses often become the focus of their people. Familiarity becomes a devastating trap. Yet, another minister can enter the pulpit preaching the same identical message, and the people respond greatly. Familiarity has not yet raised its ugly head. My father often had evangelists come and preach the same message he preached. Yet, the people would say, "Wow! We've never heard any preaching on this!" Board members who oppose every plan and vision of their leader will pay dearly for this rebellion.

The wives of men of God who fail to discern the anointing on their own husband will lose great benefits and blessings if *familiarity blinds them*.

The children of preachers who cannot differentiate between their daddy and "the man of God" may rebel and face the consequences of it.

4 Suggestions For Ministers

1. Conduct Yourself As A Man Or Woman Of God...At All Times. Do not permit the comfortable atmosphere of a cafe to break your focus on the glory, greatness and purity of our God. Do not permit the joking and the bantering of others to remove the holy atmosphere around you.

2. Never Tell Off-Color Jokes Nor Laugh With Those Who Do. After service one night, I went out to eat with a famous man of God and his entourage. Somebody asked one of the other ministers to tell a specific joke to me. He replied, "I just don't believe Mike would enjoy that kind of joke." Others looked expectantly at me. They supposed I would say, "Sure! It's just us men here. I'll understand."

I looked at the minister and said quietly, "I always want to hear anything that will increase my passion for Jesus." The table fell silent. Eventually, conversation resumed in another direction. Keep the standard high...regardless of those present.

3. Remember You Have Two Natures— The One You Decide To Feed Will Become Strongest. The golf course should not be a place where your weakness is fed, sin is encouraged and godly living is forgotten.

4. Assess The Maturity Of Those Around You Continually. David behaved himself "wisely" before the people: It did not mean that he was two-faced, but he recognized the behavior that others would interpret properly.

Every *conversation* sends a *message.*

Every *joke* sends a *message.*

Recognition of a Man or a Woman of God is vital for your total success. When God wants to bless you, He will schedule a man of God into your life. It is your responsibility to discern them, respect them and follow their instructions. "Believe in the Lord your God, so shall ye be established; believe His prophets, so shall ye prosper," (2 Chronicles 20:20).

Unbelief destroys you. "If ye will not believe, surely ye shall not be established," (Isaiah 7:9).

Recognition Of A Man Of God Will Birth Instant Miracles, Dramatic Changes And Prevent A Thousand Tragedies In Your Life.

RECOMMENDED BOOKS AND TAPES ON THIS TOPIC

B-12 The Minister's Encyclopedia, 3 Vols. (890 pages/$90)
B-82 31 Reasons People Do Not Receive Their Financial Harvest (252 pages/$12)
B-90 The Gift of Wisdom for Ministers (32 pages/$10)
B-91 The Leadership Secrets of Jesus (196 pages/$10)
B-107 The Uncommon Minister, Vol. 1 (32 pages/$5)
B-108 The Uncommon Minister, Vol. 2 (32 pages/$5)
B-109 The Uncommon Minister, Vol. 3 (32 pages/$5)
B-110 The Uncommon Minister, Vol. 4 (32 pages/$5)
B-111 The Uncommon Minister, Vol. 5 (32 pages/$5)
B-112 The Uncommon Minister, Vol. 6 (32 pages/$5)
B-113 The Uncommon Minister, Vol. 7 (32 pages/$5)
TS-38 31 Reasons People Do Not Receive Their Financial Harvest (6 tapes/$30)

☙ 13 ☙

RECOGNITION OF YOUR DOMINANT GIFT

➤◦❖◦◄

Everyone Receives Gifts From God.
Few recognize their *dominant* gift.
David recognized his dominant gift. He was more than a singer. He was more than a shepherd boy. He was a warrior and he knew it. That is why he recognized an opportunity for his gift to flourish when Goliath cursed his God.

Joseph knew his dominant gift. He was more than an interpreter of dreams. In fact, The Scriptures only document two or three occasions of it. His gift was uncommon compassion. That gift caused him to recognize the countenance of the butler and the baker in the prison. Their unhappiness was the Golden Hinge to his ascent to the throne. I love what my dear friend Sherman Owens always teaches: "Listen to happy voices for *encouragement*; listen to unhappy voices for *ideas.*"

The Apostle Paul knew his dominant gift. "I am called an apostle..." He was more than a thinker. He was more than a talker. His gift was to reveal the revelation of God.

14 Facts You Should Know About Your Gifts And Talents

1. Jesus Wanted Us To Recognize That God Gives Wonderful Gifts To Us. "If ye then, being evil, know how to give good gifts unto your children, how much more shall your Father which is in Heaven give good things to them that ask Him?" (Matthew 7:11).

2. The Holy Spirit Gives You All The Gifts, Talents And Abilities You Possess. "Now there are diversities of gifts, but the same Spirit," (1 Corinthians 12:4).

3. The Holy Spirit Gives Different Gifts To Us, Relative To Our Assignment On Earth. "But all these worketh that one and the selfsame Spirit, dividing to every man severally as he will. For as the body is one, and hath many members, and all the members of that one body, being many, are one body: so also is Christ," (1 Corinthians 12:11-12).

4. Your Gifts Were Given To Help Men Of God Fulfill Their Instructions And Vision From God. "Then wrought Bezaleel and Aholiab, and every wise hearted man, in whom the Lord put wisdom and understanding to know how to work all manner of work for the service of the sanctuary, according to all that the Lord had commanded. And Moses called Bezaleel and Aholiab, and every wise hearted man, in whose heart the Lord had put wisdom, even every one whose heart stirred him up to come unto the work to do it," (Exodus 36:1-2).

5. Your Gift Was Imparted To You To Solve

Problems For Those Closest To You. "Withhold not good from them to whom it is due, when it is in the power of thine hand to do it," (Proverbs 3:27).

6. When Your Dominant Gift Becomes Your Seed In The Lives Of Others, God Guarantees To Generously Compensate You. "Knowing that whatsoever good thing any man doeth, the same shall he receive of the Lord, whether he be bond or free," (Ephesians 6:8).

7. Few Ever Recognize Their Dominant Gift. This explains why millions live life unrewarded for the gift they contain. Nothing is more tormenting than living life uncelebrated for the difference within you.

8. Obsession With Your Flaws Will Often Blind You To Your Dominant Gift. We study ourselves. As we stand before a mirror each morning, we rehearse the qualities that discourage us the most. It is a costly exercise. Marilyn Hickey, my longtime friend, shared an interesting experience. She had just returned from China. When I finished speaking at their church in Denver, Colorado, she leaned over and told me this story. China has the greatest ping-pong players on earth. So, she asked the master Mentors of their champions how they handled the weaknesses of their Protegés. They explained that they ignore them, choosing rather to spend all of their teaching time on developing their dominant trait or gift to its highest level possible. They explained that if the dominant strength of a player received total focus, it would compensate for any weakness elsewhere in their form.

9. Your Dominant Gift Will Operate Well

In A Hostile Environment. A brilliant young boxer said, "The greater the challenge, the more energy arises within me." A house painter may receive $15 an hour, but if you bring him 50 floors high on a skyscraper, his income will multiply. *An adversarial atmosphere will always magnify the rewards possible through your gift.* Stop thinking your gift cannot be used because of a climate of hostility around you. It will magnify the reward of it like David was rewarded for killing Goliath.

10. The Focus Of Others Often Distorts Our Personal Awareness Of Our Dominant Gift. Our families and relatives may study our flaws from childbirth. Our weakness becomes their focus. Unfortunately, we adapt to it. We start looking at the thing they despise.

11. Admiration Of Others With Different Gifts Often Blinds Us Toward Our Own Dominant Gift. It happened with me as a young boy. Everyone honored my father. My mother continuously expressed her respect and admiration. Daddy was quiet while I was growing up. Seven of us kids remember a very quiet, non-talkative father at the table. So, since he was the idol of those I loved, he became my idol. I wanted to be like Daddy. Well, my personality was quite different. I talked a lot. In fact, I made very low grades in conduct in school throughout my 12 years! But it appeared that quietness was magnetic. Everyone loved a quiet person, it seemed. So, I wrote Scriptures out on 3 x 5 index cards, emphasizing the importance of silence. "Set a watch before my mouth..." "Study to be quiet..." Every time I felt the urge to talk in a group of people, I pulled my cards out. I read them feverishly and intensely. I wanted to be "a quiet person" more than anything else I knew.

It became more than I could bear.

Finally, I screamed out to my mother, "Mother, I have got to talk!"

She suggested something nobody else had ever thought about. "Son, maybe there is a gift involved. Now, we have got to pray and ask the Lord to give you something to say that folks would not mind listening to." That birthed my obsession for substance and essence in every conversation.

12. Your Gift Will Be Removed From You Unless You Use It. "Take therefore the talent from him, and give it unto him which hath ten talents...cast ye the unprofitable servant into outer darkness: there shall be weeping and gnashing of teeth," (Matthew 25:28, 30).

13. What You Would Love To Do Most Every Day Of Your Life Is A Clue To Your Dominant Gift. If money were *not* involved, if convenience were not the consideration, what would you *attempt* to do with your life?

Here is a little test:

If every human on earth were only permitted to receive $10 per hour for working (taxicab driver or the President of the United States), what would you want to do every day for the rest of your life?

14. Your Significance Is Not In Your Similarity To Another But In Your Point Of Difference From Another. You did not marry your husband because he reminded you of a previous boyfriend. He was *unlike* your old boyfriend. You do not attend your local church because it reminds you of one across town. It is *unlike* the one across town.

Celebrate Your Difference.

It is wonderful to learn from others. Implement their knowledge and skills when possible. But, it destroys your difference and significance if you fail to recognize that your own *dominant* gift has been given to you from God for a different purpose.

Uncommon Men Are Simply Common Men Who Have Recognized Their Uncommon Gift.

Recognition Of Your Dominant Gift Can Move You From Obscurity To Significance In A Day.

RECOMMENDED BOOKS AND TAPES ON THIS TOPIC

B-05 Finding Your Purpose in Life (32 pages/$3)

B-09 Four Forces That Guarantee Career Success (32 pages/$3)

B-73 The Mentor's Manna on Abilities (32 pages/$3)

B-74 The Assignment: The Dream & The Destiny, Vol. 1 (164 pages/$10)

B-75 The Assignment: The Anointing & The Adversity, Vol. 2 (192 pages/$10)

B-100 The Holy Spirit Handbook, Vol. 1 (153 pages/$10)

TS-18 The Double Diamond Principle in Gifts, Goals and Greatness (6 tapes/$30)

TS-24 31 Secrets of the Uncommon Problem-Solver (6 tapes/$30)

TS-29 The Holy Spirit Handbook (6 tapes/$30)

TS-52 The Assignment: The Dream & The Destiny (6 tapes/$30)

∾ 14 ∾

RECOGNITION OF YOUR DOMINANT WEAKNESS

━━━━━━━━▶━◉━◀━━━━━━━━

Every Human Contains Weaknesses.

God has anticipated every weakness. "For He remembered that they were but flesh; a wind that passeth away, and cometh not again" (Psalm 78:39).

One Weakness can *destroy* you.

Your refusal to recognize it guarantees your destruction.

Recognition of your *dominant* weakness can save you a thousand nights of tears, failure and devastation. Brilliant, articulate and powerful people have permitted a tiny weakness to eat away like a small cancer. *Things that begin small can become huge.* Greed, lust, lying, prayerlessness and even gossip can grow until that weakness becomes a raging inferno.

You cannot afford to ignore your dominant weakness. Your weakness is like a living person within you, a living organism. It is a force, silent and deadly, that moves your life toward destruction. If ignored, it will wreck every dream, sabotage every worthy relationship and ultimately make you a monument of disgrace on the earth.

17 Important Facts You Should Remember About Your Weakness

1.   Everyone Has A Weakness. "All have sinned," (Romans 3:23). Many camouflage their weakness. Always remember that those around you contain a weakness, too. Failure to discern theirs can destroy you as well.

2.   Your Heavenly Father Is Fully Aware Of Your Personal Weakness. It matters to Him. He cares. He longs to give you the strength to destroy it. "For He remembered that they were but flesh," (Psalm 78:39). "He remembereth that we are dust," (Psalm 103:14).

3.   Your Weakness Is The Entry Point For Demonic Spirits. Satan *entered* Judas (John 13:26).

4.   God Will Make Every Effort To Reveal Your Weakness To You Before It Destroys You. "And the Lord said, Simon, Simon, behold, satan hath desired to have you, that he may sift you as wheat," (Luke 22:31).

5.   Somebody Will Be Assigned By Hell To Feed And Strengthen Your Weakness. Delilah was sent by satan to destroy Samson (Judges 16:4-5).

6.   Your Weakness Will Pursue, Embrace And Seize Any Friendship That Permits It, Feeds On It Or Enjoys It. The contentious spirit in one person can infiltrate an entire church through those who allow it to exist unrebuked, unchecked or uncorrected.

7.   Your Weakness Has An Agenda, A Plan To Take Over Your Life And Sabotage It. "When lust hath conceived, it bringeth forth sin: and sin, when it is finished, bringeth forth death," (James 1:15).

8. Your Weakness Will Bond You With Wrong People. Remember Samson and Delilah! (See Judges 16:4-20.)

9. Your Weakness Will Separate You From Right People. Adam withdrew from God in the garden after he sinned. Your weakness makes you uncomfortable in the presence of those who refuse to justify it (Genesis 3:8).

10. Your Weakness Can Emerge At Any Time In Your Life, Including Your Closing Years. "Cast me not off in the time of old age; forsake me not when my strength faileth," (Psalm 71:9). I think it was Dr. Lester Summrall who once said, *"What you fail to master in your early years will master you in your later years."* It is true—what you fail to conquer in your early youth will destroy you in the closing years of your life.

11. Your Weakness Cannot Be Overcome With Humanism, Human Philosophy, Explanations Or Self Will-Power. If your weakness could be overcome by yourself, the blood of Jesus is powerless and The Holy Spirit is unnecessary. "Ye shall receive power, after that the Holy Ghost is come upon you," (Acts 1:8).

12. Your Weakness Does Not Necessarily Require A Personal Confession To Everybody, But Recognition Of It In The Presence Of God. (See Psalm 34:18 and James 5:16.)

13. The Easiest Time To Destroy Your Weakness Is At Its Beginning Stages. Time weaves a steel thread that *becomes* an unbreakable chain. Thousands today hate the very cigarettes they are smoking, but time has enslaved them.

14. God Will Permit You To Enjoy Many Victories Even While Your Weakness Is Operating Within You. He is long-suffering. He is merciful. He provides opportunity after opportunity to reach for deliverance (see Matthew 23:37).

15. Those You Love Are Waiting In The Shadows For You To Overcome And Triumph Over Your Weakness. Your victory sends a message to them. When David killed Goliath, the entire nation of Israel changed its season. Your family may be sitting in constant fear that your weakness will destroy you and them. They may be fearful that their own weakness will be exposed. But, when you become victorious, their hearts rejoice and will become strengthened because of it.

16. Your Weakness Can Only Be Overcome By The Word Of God. Satan reacts to The Word of God. That is why Jesus used the weapon of The Word during His temptation (read Matthew 4:1-11).

17. Overcoming Your Weakness Will Bring You An Incredible Reward For Eternity. (See Revelation 3.)

What is the most dominant weakness in your life that satan has consistently used to dilute your testimony, break your focus and create depression? You may hide it for a season, but time exposes all things.

Address your weakness.

Become an enemy to it. Trust The Holy Spirit to empower you.

Confession is evidence of trust.

10 Wisdom Keys To Remember

1. What You Fail To Destroy Will Eventually Destroy You. God told Saul to destroy all the Amalekites. He permitted King Agag to live. At his death, it was a young warrior Amalekite that took the credit for completing his suicide and murder.

2. What You Are Willing To Walk Away From Determines What God Will Bring To You. Ruth walked away from Moab and met Boaz, the Uncommon Husband. Judas refused to walk away from the money offered to him for the betrayal of Jesus. He committed suicide.

3. All Men Fall—The Great Ones Get Back Up. Your weakness can be overcome. Even when you have failed, get back up.

4. Stop Looking At Where You Have Been And Start Looking At Where You Are Going. Yesterday is over. Talk like it. Speak words that move you toward your future instead of your past.

5. You Cannot Correct What You Are Unwilling To Confront. Face your weakness. If you ignore it, it grows.

6. Crisis Always Occurs At The Curve Of Change. Sometimes, when we make major changes in our career, our home or our plans, crisis emerges. Our weaknesses surface. Discern this. Look ahead.

7. Anger Is The Birthplace For Solutions. Hate your weakness. Despise it. Then, focus that anger appropriately.

8. Struggle Is The Proof That You Have Not Yet Been Conquered. You may feel that you are battling every moment of your life against your weakness. That's the proof you are still the champion, the Winner.

9. What You Can Tolerate, You Cannot Change. You cannot conquer a weakness if you keep a tolerant attitude toward it. If you think your weakness is just "a little vice and everyone is entitled to one"—it will eventually destroy you.

10. Every Relationship Will Feed A Weakness Or A Strength In You. Name relationships for what they really are. Do you keep someone in your life because they tolerate your weakness? Feed it? Nurture it? Wrong people breathe life into your weakness that God is attempting to kill.

Recognition Of Your Dominant Weakness Will Help You Avoid Disgrace, Loss And Tragedy.

RECOMMENDED BOOKS AND TAPES ON THIS TOPIC

B-02   Five Steps Out of Depression (32 pages/$3)
B-03   The Sex Trap (32 pages/$5)
B-07   Battle Techniques for War-Weary Saints (32 pages/$5)
B-17   Seeds of Wisdom on Overcoming (32 pages/$3)
B-18   Seeds of Wisdom on Habits (32 pages/$3)
B-21   Seeds of Wisdom on Adversity (32 pages/$3)
B-23   Seeds of Wisdom on Prayer (32 pages/$3)
B-29   The Survival Bible (248 pages/$10)
B-40   Wisdom for Crisis Times (112 pages/$9)
B-48   31 Keys to a New Beginning (32 pages/$5)
B-56   How to Turn Your Mistakes into Miracles (32 pages/$5)
B-69   Wisdom Keys for a Powerful Prayer Life (32 pages/$3)
B-115 Seeds of Wisdom on The Secret Place (32 pages/$5)
TS-40 Wisdom for Crisis Times (6 tapes/$30)

≈ 15 ≈

RECOGNITION OF THE DOMINANT GIFT IN OTHERS

Greatness Is Within Those You Love.

You must *find* it. You must *focus* on it. You must *see* it as the gift of God to you.

Everything you do not have has been carefully stored in someone near you.

Love is the secret map to that treasure.

One of the major mistakes in my life happened many years ago. A young lady worked for me who was incredibly spontaneous, happy and joyful. When she walked into a room, *everything smiled.* Her gift was enthusiasm. She headed my music company.

One day, I pulled open the filing cabinets. Everything was in disarray. Bank statements had been misfiled and labeled. It looked like a catastrophe. Upset, I called her into my office.

"I love you very much. You are very special to me, but I cannot have disorder in my office. I suggest that you go to Bible School. I will pay your way through Bible College. I know you love God and God has His hand on your life."

She cried. I cried. For weeks afterwards, it was like my office was a funeral home. I never realized my staff was so boring until she left! It was like death in the place.

Months later, it dawned on me. I wanted her to be a *coach* but God had given her the personality of a *cheerleader*.

She was a *motivator*, not an educator.

Her gift was *joy*, not judgment.

Her gift was *spontaneity*, not structure.

Her gift was *enthusiasm*, not efficiency.

Since then, I have tried hard to search for the dominant core gift of those near me. It is important to *feed* that gift, *build* on that gift and not become preoccupied with their weakness. Your circle of friends can offer you motivation, mentorship, correction, loyalty or celebration. Nobody contains it *all*.

4 Keys That Strengthen Friendships

1. Everything You Need Or Want Is Hidden In Someone Near You. God stores His Heavenly treasure in earthen vessels.

2. What You Respect Will Move Toward You. When you respect someone's gift, your enthusiasm will be apparent. They will respond to you.

3. When God Wants To Bless You, He Places A Person In Your Life. God knows how to staff your weakness. What you do not have, He has placed near you. It is your responsibility to respect and *find it*.

4. Someone Is Always Observing You Who Is Capable Of Greatly Blessing You. Someone is watching you struggle. Someone knows you are having difficulties. They could solve your problems swiftly and quickly...if you would reach out toward them.

What Blinds Us To The Gifts Of Others?

Failure to recognize the dominant gift in others can occur when we become obsessed with their flaws, self-absorbed with our own goals and overloaded with unreasonable schedules.

Several years ago, I went to a friend's home. I enjoyed him and loved being around him. Externally, his home was gorgeous. It had wealth written all over it. But, when I entered the home, it was almost like a pigpen. It was dirty, cluttered, disorganized and even the refrigerator had dirty handprints all over it. When he started preparing me a sandwich, I declined. "Brother, this is too bad in here. I just can't eat in this kind of an atmosphere. In fact, your house needs cleaning bad!!"

He was embarrassed greatly. "I know. My wife refuses to keep it clean. I pay for this house, pay the light bill and the water bill and it seems to me that the least she can do is to keep it clean." He was exasperated, embarrassed and humiliated by it.

"How long have you been married?" I asked.

"Twenty years."

"I have a prophetic word for you, Brother! She is *not* going to clean this house! *Ever!* If you have been married 20 years and she still keeps a dirty house, it is not her gift nor desire to do so."

"But, that is her Scriptural responsibility!" He was fuming.

"Not really," I said. "You can stretch that little phrase "keeper of the home" as long as you want to, but you cannot find Scriptural proof that it is the woman's responsibility to vacuum her house, make up the beds and clean out toilets. That is a *cultural expectation,* not a Scriptural command," I said.

I explained further. "You hate housework. She hates housework. There are people who *love* housework. It is their business. I have two ladies that have been a great blessing to my own life in cleaning my house," I explained.

Then, I asked him another question. "How long does it take you to make $150?"

"About one-and-a-half hours," he answered. He was a salesman.

"I want to do something for you. I want to pay the two ladies who clean my house to clean your house for three days. It will take at least that long to get it decent. The reason I want to pay to do this is so you will have a *memory* of how beautiful a home can be when it's clean and in order. I want you to work an extra one-and-a-half hours each month to make 150 extra dollars. Take the 150 extra dollars to have your house cleaned."

I asked him serious questions. "Why did you marry your wife? What did you love most about her? What was her attraction to you?" *The dominant attraction determines the longevity of the relationship.*

"I love her laughter. She always laughs at my jokes. She is so much fun to be with. I love to take her places," was his reply.

"Then, while these two ladies are cleaning your house on one cleaning day every month, take your wife out to eat! Sit her on your lap in the backyard! Hug and kiss her or tell her the jokes that she loves and enjoys. But don't make her do things that she hates to do when you can provide that for her and free her time to enjoy your presence!"

Some of us have not recognized the uncommon *difference* and dominant gift in those nearest us. It has cost us dearly.

Recognition Of The Dominant Gift In Others Will Multiply The Joy You Receive From Them.

RECOMMENDED BOOKS AND TAPES ON THIS TOPIC

B-14 Seeds of Wisdom on Relationships (32 pages/$3)

B-49 The Proverbs 31 Woman (70 pages/$7)

B-57 Thirty-One Secrets of an Unforgettable Woman (140 pages/$9)

B-74 The Assignment: The Dream & The Destiny, Vol. 1 (164 pages/$10)

B-75 The Assignment: The Anointing & The Adversity, Vol. 2 (192 pages/$10)

B-95 Secrets of The Journey, Vol. 4 (32 pages/$5)

B-97 The Assignment: The Trials & The Triumph, Vol. 3 (160 pages/$10)

B-98 The Assignment: The Pain & The Passion, Vol. 4 (144 pages/$10)

B-99 Secrets of the Richest Man Who Ever Lived (179 pages/$10)

TS-16 The Double Diamond Principle in Successful Relationships (6 tapes/$30)

TS-25 Secrets of the Richest Man Who Ever Lived (6 tapes/$30)

TS-52 The Assignment: The Dream & The Destiny (6 tapes/$30)

TS-53 Thirty-One Secrets of an Unforgettable Woman (6 tapes/$30)

**"Wherefore let him that thinketh he
standeth take heed lest he fall."
1 Corinthians 10:12**

☞ 16 ☜

RECOGNITION OF THE DOMINANT WEAKNESS OF THOSE YOU HAVE CHOSEN TO TRUST

━━━━━━━➤ੇ੦ੇ◄━━━━━━

Weakness Is Contagious.

Conduct *Allowed* Becomes Conduct *Approved.*

Every day, the newspaper is full of illustrations and reports regarding a high school student that was "in the wrong place at the wrong time with the wrong people." Recently, a mother shared how her son was in a car containing drugs. He had never taken drugs in his life, but he was friendly and a companion to those who did. The police stopped them. Every one of them received a jail sentence, including her son.

You cannot afford to ignore the weaknesses of those near you.

Jonah is a fascinating story of a rebellious preacher. He paid the fare on a ship going to a different destination than God had commanded. The judgments of God followed him.

Rebels are always penalized.

Always.

The ship almost capsized. The wrath of God

had been stirred. Jonah was on that ship. God was bringing pressure on him to repent and make a change. Those who permitted his presence were exposed to the same wrath and judgment. When they threw Jonah overboard, the consequences of his rebellion were not felt any longer. Calm came. You see, you do not have to be Jonah for the storm to affect your life.

When you tolerate the presence of those who are rebellious against God, you will taste the same results and consequences. Korah rebelled against the authority of Moses. But, when the judgment came, 250 people were destroyed with him—his family.

It is important that you know the weaknesses of those nearest you.

You Must Recognize The Dominant Weakness Of Your Mate. Satan will attack your life...through your mate. One minister once told me, "I refused to face the fact that my wife enjoyed the atmosphere of the ungodly. She loved the climate of casinos, ungodly music and dirty jokes. It eventually destroyed our marriage."

You Must Recognize The Dominant Weakness Of Your Children. My mother searched between mattresses, in closet boxes and everywhere...to find magazines or anything that would confirm her suspicions in us boys. I said, "Mother, don't you trust me?"

"Not a lick," was her usual reply.

She was aware that any weakness in the children would infiltrate and penetrate the climate of our home. Everything Changes When A Weakness Is Permitted To Grow Close To You.

You Must Recognize The Dominant Weakness Of

Those Who Work With You. When a young man I dearly loved misrepresented a price to one of my vendors, I had to fire him. He explained that he was trying to make me money, save on a bill. But, I realized that if he would lie to help me, eventually he would lie about me. One of the greatest Wisdom Keys I ever discovered was—*Those Who Sin With You Will Eventually Sin Against You.*

You Must Recognize The Dominant Weakness In Those Handling Your Finances. I spoke to a wife whose husband continuously defrauded the government in taxes and reports. He is in prison today. She was completely oblivious to his weakness. Now, she is scraping financially to provide for her children. When you know the dominant weakness of those around you, it enables you to:

▶ *Pray appropriately and with faith.*

▶ *Prepare for the consequences.*

Everyone Trusts Someone.

Those you have chosen to *trust* hold the keys to your future.

8 Facts Concerning The Weaknesses Of Others

1. Jesus Understood The Weaknesses Of Those Close To Him. Peter had some personal problems. That is why Jesus said, "Satan hath desired to have you, that he may sift you as wheat: But I have prayed for thee, that thy faith fail not," (Luke 22:31-32). So, it is important to pray for those who are linked to you.

2. Those Who Serve Men Of God Often Have Weaknesses, Too. Look at Gehazi. Most of us would think he had too much of God's presence to lie to Naaman and request the gift that had been reserved for Elisha, but his dominant weakness surfaced (2 Kings 5:22).

Judas was continuously in the presence of Jesus. Yet, his weakness flourished (Matthew 26:47-49).

Absalom had access to the greatest warrior in history, King David. Yet, his envy and need for power overcame him (read 2 Samuel 15:2-6).

3. Satan's Favorite Entry Point Into Your Life Will Always Be Through Someone Close To You. It happened in the life of Jesus, Joseph and even Paul. It can happen to you.

4. You Can Love People Without Trusting Them. I have friends that I dearly love and enjoy their company. They laugh easily. They care deeply about my life. But, I have learned not to trust them with *information,* because they are not discreet. I do not trust them with my *finances,* because they do not have the integrity to repay their own debts. When I am in their company, I enjoy their laughter, their climate of ease and fun, but my love for them does not require my trusting them.

5. Some People Are Trustworthy, But Not Enjoyable. You will have people in your life that will do exactly what they say. They will not destroy you. They will not damage your life, but they do not share your goals and dreams. Your successes activate their rivalry, not their admiration of you.

6. Discern Where Satan Has Previously Deceived Those You Love. One friend had a drug problem. He had mastered it. He traveled everywhere. So, he came and spent some time assisting me in my ministry. I was horrified to find out that several times when he had worked for me, he had taken drugs. Knowing that was still his weakness would have prepared me more for the shocking experience I encountered later.

7. The Weakness Of Others Often Flourishes In The Presence Of Certain Friends. Know those friends. Know when they accompany each other to parties, vacations or routine outings.

8. Someone You Trust Will Always Trust Someone Else You Would Not. I have experienced broken confidences more often than I like to recall. The deception of *friendliness,* the trap of *familiarity* and the climate of *fatigue* has destroyed many friendships.

8 Important Suggestions When You Recognize The Dominant Weakness Of Those You Love

1. Do Not Permit Your Imagination Or Suspicious Nature To Magnify Their Weakness More Than What It Really Is. Conversations and gossip can turn tiny sparks into huge forest fires very easily. Jealousy, envy and lying spirits have destroyed many homes. A lying spirit reveals itself when you consistently find yourself looking or expecting another to fail. *Satan turns something small into something huge within your mind.*

2. Intercede For That Person To God. Jesus prayed for Peter and the results came. Prayer works. Ask The Holy Spirit to give you the words that will properly address the problem.

3. Talk Directly To The Person About Their Weakness. If they confess it, you have created a prayer partner and possible friend. If they rebel, you have exposed them as a fool. Only God can change them from that point.

4. Insist On Praying With Them Concerning Their Weakness. Without The Holy Spirit, every one of us will fail anyway. Invite God to get involved.

5. Find The Testimonies Of Overcomers Who Have Defeated That Same Weakness In Their Lives. Purchase the book or share the testimony with your friend.

6. Keep The Confidentiality Of Their Weakness Forever Between You And God. It is the glory of a king "to conceal a matter."

Discretion is honorable.

Confidentiality will be ultimately rewarded.

Silence provides God a season to intervene and create changes.

7. Evaluate Your Own Personal Weaknesses During This Season And Permit Humility To Be Produced Because Of It. When we discern the weaknesses of others, it is an appropriate time to address the weaknesses within ourselves. Believe that God will sow mercy toward you as you sow mercy toward others.

Unfounded suspicions become entry points for lying spirits. Reject the temptation to magnify or grow an offense or a hidden fear. "Wherefore let him that thinketh he standeth take heed lest he fall," (1 Corinthians 10:12).

8. Depend On God To Get Involved. "There hath no temptation taken you but such as is common to man: but God is faithful, Who will not suffer you to be tempted above that ye are able; but will with the temptation also make a way to escape, that ye may be able to bear it," (1 Corinthians 10:13).

▶ "We then that are strong ought to bear the infirmities of the weak, and not to please ourselves," (Romans 15:1).

▶ "Who art thou that judgest another man's servant? to his own master he standeth or falleth. Yea, he shall be holden up: for God is able to make him stand," (Romans 14:4).

▶ "Brethren, if a man be overtaken in a fault, ye which are spiritual, restore such an one in the spirit of meekness; considering thyself, lest thou also be tempted. Bear ye one another's burdens, and so fulfil the law of Christ," (Galatians 6:1-2).

Recognition Of The Dominant Weakness In Those You Love Will Reduce Expectations And Breathe Longevity And Loyalty Into The Friendship.

RECOMMENDED BOOKS AND TAPES ON THIS TOPIC
B-14   Seeds of Wisdom on Relationships (32 pages/$3)
B-19   Seeds of Wisdom on Warfare (32 pages/$3)
B-21   Seeds of Wisdom on Adversity (32 pages/$3)
B-40   Wisdom for Crisis Times (112 pages/$9)
B-58   The Mentor's Manna on Attitude (32 pages/$3)
TS-03   How to Walk Through Fire (6 tapes/$30)
TS-40   Wisdom for Crisis Times (6 tapes/$30)

"And he said unto Jesus, Lord, remember me when Thou comest into Thy kingdom."
Luke 23:42

❧ 17 ❧

RECOGNITION OF GREATNESS WHEN YOU ENTER ITS PRESENCE

Greatness Is Usually Camouflaged.

Few recognized Jesus "in swaddling clothes" in a manger. Few recognized Him in the Temple as the Son of God.

Two thieves died next to Christ at the crucifixion. One did *not* recognize who He was and cursed Him. The other *recognized* Him...and requested "...remember me," (Luke 23:42).

Several years ago, a man that I respect and admire very much gave me this secret.

"Mike, never permit greatness in your presence without celebrating it, recognizing it and acknowledging it in some way." Then, I observed him. If an incredible athlete was eating in the same restaurant, my friend would write him a note of gratitude or even pick up his restaurant tab on the way out. Today, my friend is seen in magazines with the greatest names in human influence. Kings, presidents of nations and the greatest leaders of our world are with him on a regular basis.

He cultivated the habit of recognizing

greatness whenever he saw it.

The Scriptures are full of examples of greatness.

Some had great *Faith.*

Some had great *Endurance.*

Some had great *Giftings.*

Some had great *Influence.*

Some had great *Wisdom.*

Jonathan recognized greatness in David. Some sons often see greatness overlooked by their fathers. Saul never saw it in David.

The servant of Abraham discerned the greatness of Rebekah. He had asked the Lord to reveal the mate of Isaac. "And let it come to pass, that the damsel to whom I shall say, Let down thy pitcher, I pray thee, that I may drink; and she shall say, Drink, and I will give thy camels drink also: let the same be she that thou hast appointed for thy servant Isaac," (Genesis 24:14).

Ruth discerned the greatness of Naomi. It linked her to Boaz, the financial champion of Bethlehem.

Abigail recognized the greatness of David. He avoided the bloodshed of Nabal because of it. Abigail later became the wife of David.

6 Things You Should Remember About Greatness

1. Greatness Is Not The Absence Of Weakness. You see, everyone has weaknesses. Job said, "Great men are not always wise," (Job 32:9)

2. All Men Fall, The Great Ones Get Back Up. When you think of greatness, do not think of unmarred, unscarred, unbattered and perfect human specimens. Everyone has scars— invisible or visible. Scarred generals *inspire* the troops.

3. Fathers Sometimes See Greatness Ignored By Their Sons. David recognized the unforgettable loyalty of Jonathan.

4. What You Respect, You Will Attract. What you respect will come toward you. What you do not respect will move away from you. It does not matter if it is a miracle, a dog or a person!

5. Greatness Is When Someone Walks Away From The Temptation Of Pleasure To Protect Their Integrity. Joseph never sought to retaliate against Potiphar's wife. On the other side of the door of pain is promotion.

6. Greatness Is When Someone Willingly Confronts An Enemy Nobody Else Wants To Fight. David is an example. When King Saul and David's own brothers were afraid, David willingly confronted their enemy, Goliath.

Recognition Of Greatness Guarantees When You Enter Its Presence.

RECOMMENDED BOOKS AND TAPES ON THIS TOPIC

B-39   The Double Diamond Principle (148 pages/$9)
B-49   The Proverbs 31 Woman (70 pages/$7)
B-57   Thirty-One Secrets of an Unforgettable Woman (140 pages/$9)
B-68   The Gift of Wisdom for Achievers (32 pages/$10)
B-99   Secrets of the Richest Man Who Ever Lived (179 pages/$10)
B-104 7 Keys to 1000 Times More (128 pages/$10)
TS-06   Secrets of the Greatest Achievers Who Ever Lived, Series 1 (6 tapes/$30)
TS-07   Secrets of the Greatest Achievers Who Ever Lived, Series 2 (6 tapes/$30)
TS-18   The Double Diamond Principle in Gifts, Goals and Greatness (6 tapes/$30)
TS-25   Secrets of the Richest Man Who Ever Lived (6 tapes/$30)
TS-30   7 Keys to 1000 Times More (6 tapes/$30)
TS-37   31 Secrets of the Uncommon Mentor (6 tapes/$30)
TS-53   31 Secrets of an Unforgettable Woman (6 tapes/$30)

"Behold, I have dreamed a dream
more; and, behold, the sun and the
moon and the eleven stars made
obeisance to me."
Genesis 37:9

☞ 18 ☜

RECOGNITION OF THE UNCOMMON DREAM THAT ENERGIZES YOU

God Communicates Through Pictures.
He communicated with Abraham with a picture.
"That in blessing I will bless thee, and in multiplying I will multiply thy seed as the stars of the Heaven, and as the sand which is upon the sea shore; and thy seed shall possess the gate of his enemies," (Genesis 22:17).

He communicated to Joseph with a picture in a dream. "Behold, I have dreamed a dream more; and, behold, the sun and the moon and the eleven stars made obeisance to me," (Genesis 37:9).

At some time, God will birth within you an invisible picture of your future. That *Uncommon Dream* will be something you can *do,* something you can *become* or something you can *have.* God uses this Uncommon Dream to provide focus, progression and enthusiasm.

Satan will develop a strategy to *cloud* this picture and paralyze this Uncommon Dream.

You must recognize the Dream that God uses to stir hope, inspire direction and make you a blessing to others.

24 Powerful Facts About The Uncommon Dream Within You

1. You Must Continually Visualize This Uncommon Dream In Your Heart And Mind. "Write the vision, and make it plain upon tables, that he may run that readeth it," (Habakkuk 2:2).

2. An Uncommon Dream Will Require Uncommon Patience. "For the vision is yet for an appointed time, but at the end it shall speak, and not lie: though it tarry, wait for it; because it will surely come, it will not tarry," (Habakkuk 2:3).

3. God Is Committed To The Uncommon Dream He Is Birthing, Whether You Embrace It Yet Or Not. Peter made continuous mistakes. But Jesus said, "I have prayed for thee, that thy faith fail not: and when thou art converted, strengthen thy brethren," (Luke 22:32).

4. An Uncommon Dream Is Often Birthed From Uncommon Pain. Those raised in poverty often develop a passion for prosperity. Those with childhood disease become obsessed in helping others develop great health.

5. An Uncommon Dream Will Require Uncommon Faith. Read the biographies of uncommon men and women. Those with uncommon achievements nurtured The Seed of Faith until it became a raging Force within them.

6. The Uncommon Dream Must Be Born Within You, Not Borrowed From Others. Others have opinions, but you have direction. You alone will receive the confirmation from God for the achieving of the Dream He has birthed. Joseph had nobody else to encourage him—but he believed in his own Dream.

7. The Uncommon Dream Will Require Uncommon Focus. The Only Reason Men Fail Is Broken Focus. You will only succeed with something that consumes you. When God gives you The Uncommon Dream—it will require all of you, your time, your love and energy.

8. The Uncommon Dream Will Require Uncommon Passion. Passion is energy, enthusiasm and strength. Passion is a clue to the path The Holy Spirit has chosen for your life. Now, it is possible to have a passion for something that is unholy. But, it is important that you recognize that any uncommon achievement will require uncommon passion from God.

9. The Uncommon Dream Will Require Uncommon Favor With Others. Joseph received Favor from Potiphar and Pharaoh. Esther received Favor from the king. Ruth received Favor from Boaz. When the hand of God is upon you, Favor will come. Sow it. Expect it. Protect it. Respect it.

10. The Uncommon Dream Will Require Uncommon Preparation. Jesus prepared 30 years for three-and-one-half years of ministry. Some call it—short-term pain for long-term gain. Some vocations require many years of college before they are truly prepared for it.

11. The Uncommon Dream Will Qualify Those Who Deserve Access To You. Many reach for you, but it is important that you *qualify* those who deserve access. Jesus never went home with Pharisees, yet had an entire meal with Zacchaeus the tax collector.

12. The Uncommon Dream Will Birth Uncommon Habits. When a wealthy lady focused on developing the greatest company ever for women, she started writing down her plans every morning. She selected six things in the order of their priority. She was worth over $300 million at her death. You see, your Dream controls the habits you birth. When Muhammad Ali "saw himself" as heavyweight champion, he began to get up early in the morning for special roadwork. Champions are willing to do *daily* what ordinary men will only do *occasionally*.

13. An Uncommon Dream Creates Uncommon Adversaries. Nehemiah saw opposition erupt suddenly when God birthed within him the desire to rebuild the walls of Jerusalem. Whatever you decide to do, you will encounter opposition that will astound and shock you. It may come from your own family!

14. The Uncommon Dream Will Determine What You Do First Each Morning. Your obsession will control the use of your time.

15. The Uncommon Dream Is Usually The Opposite Of Your Present Circumstances. Joseph was hated and despised by his brothers. They sold him into slavery for $12.80. Yet, The Uncommon Dream within his heart was that of his brothers submitting to him. It was the opposite of his present! Abraham and Sarah were too old to have children. Yet, The Uncommon Dream from God was Isaac, the beginning of millions. It was the opposite of their present.

16. The Uncommon Dream Will Require The Miracles Of God. God will never birth a

Dream within you that is achievable without Him. He gives you The Dream to keep you connected to Him and to perpetuate His plans and desires. It will require Him to complete it.

17. An Uncommon Dream Will Always Require The Assistance Of Others. Keep a list of the top 12 people necessary to complete your Dream. God used 12 tribes to develop His Dream. Jesus used 12 disciples. The New Jerusalem even has 12 gates. Define your expectations of these 12. Plan a reward for their participation.

Dexter Yeager is one of the most uncommon men I have ever met. In his book, *Don't Let Anybody Steal Your Dream,* he writes, "The successful person associates with those who *support* his Dream." Believe it. You must develop people around you who believe in your dream.

18. The Uncommon Dream May Require Uncommon Negotiations With Others. Sam Walton did this. When he wanted to create the number one store in America, he went to his vendors and negotiated for lower prices.

19. The Uncommon Dream Will Require An Uncommon Plan. The command is not the plan. The command can take a *moment.* The plan can involve your *lifetime.* In a moment, God gave Noah an instruction to build the ark, but the instructions were specific and required precision.

20. When You Announce Your Uncommon Dream, Those Who Believe In You Will Be Encouraged And Energized To Assist You. You have given them a reason to function in your world. Define their position and release them to work!

21. When You Announce An Uncommon

Dream, Those Who Are Tempted To Oppose You May Decide To Join You Because Of Your Determination. Boldness is magnetic. It turns barriers into bridges. Weak people become strong in the presence of those who are bold.

22. When You Announce An Uncommon Dream, You Make It More Difficult To Fail. Your declaration removes the option to turn back and quit.

23. When You Announce Your Uncommon Dream, You Will Create An Instant Bond With Those Who Have Had A Similar Desire And Goal. Others want to assist you, because they believe in the same Dream.

24. An Uncommon Dream Will Require Careful And Wise Use Of Your Time. Great Dreams require much time. Become time-conscious. Make every hour produce a specific task for you.

Recognition Of A Divine And Uncommon Dream Birthed By God, Will Unlock Your Greatest Ideas, Creativity And Energy To Create A Truly Uncommon Life.

RECOMMENDED BOOKS AND TAPES ON THIS TOPIC

B-08   Enjoying the Winning Life (32 pages/$3)
B-09   Four Forces That Guarantee Career Success (32 pages/$3)
B-11   Dream Seeds (106 pages/$9)
B-13   Seeds of Wisdom on Dreams & Goals (32 pages/$3)
B-22   Seeds of Wisdom on Prosperity (32 pages/$3)
B-28   The Blessing Bible (252 pages/$10)
B-65   Born to Taste the Grapes (32 pages/$3)
B-99   Secrets of the Richest Man Who Ever Lived (179 pages/$10)
B-104 7 Keys to 1000 Times More (128 pages/$10)
TS-11 Dream Seeds (6 tapes/$30)

∼ 19 ∼

RECOGNITION OF THE ENEMY GOD WILL USE TO PROMOTE YOU

Jesus Always Had Enemies.

Scriptures reveal this in His own words.

Jesus Recognized His Enemies. "Why go ye about to kill Me?" (John 7:19). Any Uncommon Achiever must recognize an adversary.

The Common resent *The Uncommon.*

The Impure despise *The Pure.*

The Unholy hate *The Holy.*

The Lazy despise *The Diligent.*

3 Facts Jesus Revealed About Enemies

1. Jesus Expected His Disciples To Stir Up Enemies. "And ye shall be hated of all men for My name's sake," (Matthew 10:22). "The disciple is not above his master, nor the servant above his lord. It is enough for the disciple that he be as his master, and the servant as his lord. If they have called the master of the house Beelzebub, how much more shall they call them of his household?" (Matthew 10:24-25).

2. Jesus Instructed His Disciples To Anticipate Enemies. "Behold, I send you forth as sheep in the midst of wolves: be ye therefore wise as serpents, and harmless as doves," (Matthew 10:16).

3. **Jesus Warned His Disciples Ahead Of Time That Men Would Become Their Enemies.** "But beware of men: for they will deliver you up to the councils, and they will scourge you in their synagogues; And ye shall be brought before governors and kings for My sake, for a testimony against them and the Gentiles," (Matthew 10:17-18).

Jesus did not merely warn them of a devil.

Jesus warned them of *men*.

92 Facts You Should Know About Your Enemies

1. **You Will Always Have An Enemy.** Jesus knew it. "And ye shall be hated of all men for My name's sake: but he that endureth to the end shall be saved," (Matthew 10:22).

2. **Your Enemy Is Anyone Who Attempts To Sabotage The Assignment God Has For Your Life.** "Ye did run well; who did hinder you that ye should not obey the truth? This persuasion cometh not of Him that calleth you. A little leaven leaveneth the whole lump," (Galatians 5:7-9). "If thy brother, the son of thy mother, or thy son, or thy daughter, or the wife of thy bosom, or thy friend, which is as thine own soul, entice thee secretly, saying, Let us go and serve other gods, which thou hast not known, thou, nor thy fathers;...Thou shalt not consent unto him, nor hearken unto him; neither shall thine eye pity him, neither shalt thou spare, neither shalt thou conceal him: But thou shalt surely kill him; thine hand shall be first upon him to put him to death, and afterwards the hand of all the people,"

(Deuteronomy 13:6, 8-9).

3. Your Enemy Is Any Person Who Resents Your Desire For Increase And The Rewards It Brings. David experienced this from his oldest brother. "And Eliab his eldest brother heard when he spake unto the men; and Eliab's anger was kindled against David, and he said, Why camest thou down hither? and with whom hast thou left *those few sheep* in the wilderness? I know thy pride, and the naughtiness of thine heart; for thou art come down that thou mightest see the battle," (1 Samuel 17:28).

4. Your Enemy Is Anyone Unhappy Over Your Progress. Nehemiah faced this. Ezra faced this. They "...hired counsellors against them, to frustrate their purpose," (Ezra 4:5).

Accusations are hurled and often believed.

Letters are written and often believed.

"Now when the copy of king Artaxerxes' letter was read before Rehum, and Shimshai the scribe, and their companions, they went up in haste to Jerusalem unto the Jews, and made them to cease by force and power. Then ceased the work of the house of God which is at Jerusalem," (Ezra 4:23-24).

5. Your Enemy Is Anyone Who Increases Or Strengthens A Personal Weakness God Is Attempting To Remove From Your Life. Delilah breathed life into the weakness of Samson. She was his Enemy (Judges 16).

6. Your Enemy Is Anyone That Attempts To Kill The Faith That God Is Birthing Within You. God may be birthing your ministry. Your vision may be exploding. Your Enemy is any person who makes any attempt to abort the emergence of that Dream, Calling or Assignment.

7. Your Enemy Is Anyone Who Would Rather Discuss Your Past Than Your Future. Yesterday is over. "Remember ye not the former things, neither consider the things of old. Behold, I will do a new thing; now it shall spring forth; shall ye knot know it? I will even make a way in the wilderness, and rivers in the desert," (Isaiah 43:18-19).

When Jesus stood at the scene of the woman caught in adultery, revelation exploded. Men were present, obsessed with her mistake, ready to stone her. But, Jesus was looking at her *future*. With one single stroke of mercy, He *removed* her past: "Neither do I condemn thee," (John 8:11). Then, in a masterful stroke of the Master Artist, He painted a portrait of her *future:* "Go, and sin no more," (John 8:11).

8. Your Enemy Is Anyone Who Weakens Your Passion For Your Future And Your Dream. The ten spies were used by the Enemy to weaken the resolve of Moses to enter Canaan. The crowd instructed the blind man to be quiet. "And many charged him that he should hold his peace: but he cried the more a great deal, Thou Son of David, have mercy on me," (Mark 10:48).

9. Your Enemy Is Anyone Who Attacks The Weak Around You. Some in your life are too weak to discern a trap. They are blinded by personality, looks or even financial blessing.

10. Your Enemy Is Sometimes Those Of Your Own Household. "And a man's foes shall be they of his own household," (Matthew 10:36).

11. Your Enemy Should Not Be Feared.

"And fear not them which kill the body, but are not able to kill the soul: but rather fear him which is able to destroy both soul and body in hell," (Matthew 10:28).

12. The Perfect Will Of God Is Your Deliverance From Your Enemy. "And that we may be delivered from unreasonable and wicked men: for all men have not faith," (2 Thessalonians 3:2).

13. The Holy Spirit Will Provide Answers Concerning Your Enemy. "But when they deliver you up, take no thought how or what ye shall speak: for it shall be given you in that same hour what ye shall speak. For it is not ye that speak, but the Spirit of your Father which speaketh in you," (Matthew 10:19-20).

14. Your Enemy Is Often Discerned Ahead Of Time By Your Mentor. Jesus prepared Peter. "And the Lord said, Simon, Simon, behold, satan hath desired to have you, that he may sift you as wheat: But I have prayed for thee, that thy faith fail not: and when thou art converted, strengthen thy brethren," (Luke 22:31-32).

15. Your Fasting Can Move The Hand Of God In Destroying Your Enemy. The Old Testament prophets knew this. "Blow the trumpet in Zion, sanctify a fast, call a solemn assembly:...And I will no more make you a reproach among the heathen:...But I will remove far off from you the northern army, and will drive him into a land barren and desolate, with his face toward the east sea, and his hinder part toward the utmost sea, and his stink shall come up, and his ill savour shall come up, because he hath done great things," (Joel 2:15, 19-20).

16. God Will Fight For You Against Your Enemy. "For the Lord your God is He that goeth with you, to fight for you against your enemies, to save you," (Deuteronomy 20:4).

17. Your Enemy Will Not Be Allowed By God To Win. "The Lord is on my side; I will not fear: what can man do unto me?" (Psalm 118:6).

18. Your Enemy Is A Natural And Necessary Part Of Your Life. "If the world hate you, ye know that it hated Me before it hated you. If ye were of the world, the world would love his own: but because ye are not of the world, but I have chosen you out of the world, therefore the world hateth you. Remember the word that I said unto you, The servant is not greater than his lord. If they have persecuted Me, they will also persecute you; if they have kept My saying, they will keep yours also. But all these things will they do unto you for My name's sake, because they know not Him that sent Me," (John 15:19-21).

19. Satan Is Your Eternal Enemy. "For we wrestle not against flesh and blood, but against principalities, against powers, against the rulers of the darkness of this world, against spiritual wickedness in high places," (Ephesians 6:12).

20. You Cannot Defeat Your Enemy In Your Own Strength. "Not that we are sufficient of ourselves to think any thing as of ourselves; but our sufficiency is of God; Who also hath made us able ministers of the new testament," (2 Corinthians 3:5-6).

21. God Expects You To Prepare Your Defense Against Your Enemy. "Finally, my brethren, be strong in the Lord, and in the power of

His might. Put on the whole armour of God, that ye may be able to stand against the wiles of the devil," (Ephesians 6:10-11).

22. Overcoming Your Enemy Is The Key To Your Rewards. "He that overcometh, the same shall be clothed in white raiment; and I will not blot out his name out of the book of life, but I will confess his name before My Father, and before His angels. Him that overcometh will I make a pillar in the temple of My God, and he shall go no more out: and I will write upon him the name of My God, and the name of the city of My God, which is new Jerusalem, which cometh down out of Heaven from My God: and I will write upon him My new name," (Revelation 3:5, 12).

23. The Spoils Of War, Not Your Enemy, Must Always Remain Your Focus. "To him that overcometh will I grant to sit with Me in My throne, even as I also overcame, and am set down with My Father in His throne," (Revelation 3:21). "But rejoice, inasmuch as ye are partakers of Christ's sufferings; that, when His glory shall be revealed, ye may be glad also with exceeding joy. If ye be reproached for the name of Christ, happy are ye; for the Spirit of glory and of God resteth upon you: on their part He is evil spoken of, but on your part He is glorified," (1 Peter 4:13-14).

24. You Will Always Have A Warfare-Companion During Every Battle With Your Enemy. "Fear not: for I have redeemed thee, I have called thee by thy name; thou art Mine. When thou passest through the waters, I will be with thee; and through the rivers, they shall not overflow thee: when thou walkest through the fire, thou shalt not be burned; neither shall the flame kindle upon thee,"

(Isaiah 43:1-2).

25. Your Enemy Provides God An Opportunity To Reveal His Commitment To You. "And He said unto me, My grace is sufficient for thee: for My strength is made perfect in weakness. Most gladly therefore will I rather glory in my infirmities, that the power of Christ may rest upon me. Therefore I take pleasure in infirmities, in reproaches, in necessities, in persecutions, in distresses for Christ's sake: for when I am weak, then am I strong," (2 Corinthians 12:9-10).

26. The Wisdom For Conquering Your Enemy Will Be Imparted In Your Secret Place Of Prayer. "For in the time of trouble He shall hide me in His pavilion: in the secret of His tabernacle shall He hide me; He shall set me up upon a rock. And now shall mine head be lifted up above mine enemies round about me: therefore will I offer in His tabernacle sacrifices of joy; I will sing, yea, I will sing praises unto the Lord," (Psalm 27:5-6).

27. You Should Never Disclose Publicly The Amount Of Any Damage Done By Your Enemy. "A fool uttereth all his mind; but a wise man keepeth it in till afterwards," (Proverbs 29:11).

28. An Uncommon Enemy Will Require Uncommon Wisdom. "If any of you lack wisdom, let him ask of God, that giveth to all men liberally, and upbraideth not; and it shall be given him," (James 1:5). "Thou through Thy commandments hast made me wiser than mine enemies: for they are ever with me," (Psalm 119:98).

29. You Should Never Reveal Your Strategy Against Your Enemy To Those Uncommitted To You And Your Cause. "A fool uttereth all his mind: but a wise man keepeth it in till afterwards," (Proverbs 29:11).

30. Your Warfare With An Enemy Is Always Seasonal. "To every thing there is a season, and a time to every purpose under the heaven: A time to kill, and a time to heal; a time to break down, and a time to build up; A time to love, and a time to hate; *a time of war,* and a time of peace," (Ecclesiastes 3:1, 3, 8).

31. Your Greatest Weapon Against Your Enemy Is The Word Of God. "And take the helmet of salvation, and the sword of the Spirit, which is the Word of God," (Ephesians 6:17).

32. The Holy Spirit Will Teach You The Principles Of Warfare Against Your Enemy. "Blessed be the Lord my strength, which teacheth my hands to war, and my fingers to fight," (Psalm 144:1).

33. You Must Enter Every Battle Against Your Enemy For The Purpose Of Bringing Glory To God. "Then said David to the Philistine, Thou comest to me with a sword, and with a spear, and with a shield: but I come to thee in the name of the Lord of hosts, the God of the armies of Israel, Whom thou hast defied. This day will the Lord deliver thee into mine hand; and I will smite thee, and take thine head from thee; and I will give the carcases of the host of the Philistines this day unto the fowls of the air, and to the wild beasts of the earth;...And all this assembly shall know that the Lord saveth not with sword and spear: for the battle is the Lord's, and He will give you into our hands," (1 Samuel 17:45-47).

34. You Should Expect To Win Every Battle Against Your Enemy. "This day will the Lord deliver thee into mine hand; and I will smite thee, and take thine head from thee; and I will give the carcases of the host of the Philistines this day unto the fowls of the air, and to the wild beasts of the earth; that all the earth may know that there is a God in Israel," (1 Samuel 17:46).

35. Your Enemy Will Be Opposed By God Even When You Feel Unable To Defend Yourself. "For the battle is not yours, but God's. Ye shall not need to fight in this battle: set yourselves, stand ye still, and see the salvation of the Lord with you, O Judah and Jerusalem: fear not, nor be dismayed; to morrow go out against them: for the Lord will be with you," (2 Chronicles 20:15, 17).

"The Lord is a man of war: the Lord is His name," (Exodus 15:3).

36. The Holy Spirit Will Demoralize And Weaken Your Enemy With Fear Towards You Before The Battle Even Begins. He did it for Rahab. "And she said unto the men, I know that the Lord hath given you the land, and that your terror is fallen upon us, and that all the inhabitants of the land faint because of you. And as soon as we had heard these things, our hearts did melt, neither did there remain any more courage in any man, because of you: for the Lord your God, He is God in Heaven above, and in earth beneath," (Joshua 2:9, 11).

37. Your Enemy Is Often Ignorant Of Your Past Victories, Which Makes Them Vulnerable And Unprepared For You. Goliath was ignorant of David's fight with the lion and the bear. The

Pharisees knew nothing of the power of Jesus. Your Enemy is *not* ready for you. Be strengthened by that.

38. Your Enemy, When Aware Of Your Past Victories, Becomes Even More Fearful Of You. In Jericho, they were aware of the parade of victories, and as Rahab said, "For we have heard how the Lord dried up the water of the Red sea for you, when ye came out of Egypt; and what ye did unto the two kings of the Amorites, that were on the other side Jordan, Sihon and Og, whom ye utterly destroyed," (Joshua 2:10).

39. The Holy Spirit Will Reveal Any Snare Prepared By Your Enemy. "Lest satan should get an advantage of us: for we are not ignorant of his devices," (2 Corinthians 2:11).

40. The Holy Spirit Within You Is More Powerful Than Any Enemy That You Will Ever Face. "Greater is He that is in you, than he that is in the world," (1 John 4:4).

41. Your Enemy Will Never Discern The Protective Wall Of Angels Surrounding You During Battle. "The angel of the Lord encampeth round about them that fear Him, and delivereth them," (Psalm 34:7).

42. Your Enemy Cannot Withstand The Weapon Of Praise During Times Of Battle. "His praise shall continually be in my mouth," (Psalm 34:1).

43. Your Enemy Reveals By His Attacks That He Is Fully Persuaded Of Your Ability To Obtain Your Goal. Your Enemy would not waste the time, ammunition, finances and effort if your dreams were impossible. Paul said, "I can do

all things through Christ which strengtheneth me,"
(Philippians 4:13). If your Enemy believes in your
future, why shouldn't you?

**44. Your Enemy Will Attack You At The
Birth Of Any Significant Season In Your Life.**
When Jesus began His *ministry,* satan launched his
greatest temptations (see Matthew 4 and Luke 4).
The crisis may occur when there is the *birth of a
champion* in your household, like the birth of Moses.
His birth activated the killing of all the newborn
children in Egypt. It may be the *birth of a miracle*
about to occur in your personal life (Daniel 9). Attack
Is Merely Proof That Your Enemy Considers Your
Assignment Very Achievable.

**45. Jesus Instructed His Disciples To Sow
Seeds Of Love, Prayer And Acts Of Kindness
Into Their Enemy.** "But I say unto you, Love your
enemies, bless them that curse you, do good to them
that hate you, and pray for them which despitefully
use you, and persecute you; That ye may be the
children of your Father which is in Heaven: for He
maketh His sun to rise on the evil and on the good,
and sendeth rain on the just and on the unjust,"
(Matthew 5:44-45).

**46. Loving Your Enemies Will Create A
Great Reward.** "For if ye love them which love you,
what reward have ye? do not even the publicans the
same?" (Matthew 5:46). "But love ye your enemies,
and do good, and lend, hoping for nothing again; and
your reward shall be great, and ye shall be the
children of the Highest: for He is kind unto the
unthankful and to the evil," (Luke 6:35).

47. Any Legal Entanglement With Your

Enemy Should Be Avoided Whenever Possible. "Agree with thine adversary quickly, whiles thou art in the way with him; lest at any time the adversary deliver thee to the judge, and the judge deliver thee to the officer, and thou be cast into prison. Verily I say unto thee, Thou shalt by no means come out thence, till thou hast paid the uttermost farthing," (Matthew 5:25-26).

48. An Enemy Causes Movement In Your Life. Without a Pharaoh, the Israelites would have adapted to Egypt. The Promised Land would have become a mere fantasy instead of a fact.

49. When God Has Used Up The Benefits Of Your Present Season, He Assigns An Enemy To Become Your Exit From That Season. Remember—The Enemy causes movement. God moves you to your next season...through an adversary, like a Pharaoh.

50. Your Enemy Is An Announcement From God That Your Present Season Has Come To A Conclusion. When Goliath entered the picture, David changed seasons from shepherd boy to warrior. His victory was an announcement that yesterday was coming to a close. Tomorrow was being birthed.

51. Your Enemy Unleashes Your Imagination. When Pharaoh increased the pain and burden on the Israelites, they began to *picture* their future...where they *wanted* to be. Canaan became their focus. The Promised Land became their new target. Pain in your present is often necessary to give birth to the dream God is developing.

52. Your Enemy Exposes Your Weaknesses.

Awareness of your weakness births humility.
Humility is the magnet that attracts God and angels.

53. Your Enemy Reveals Your Limitations.
When you recognize your personal limitations you
begin looking for the solution in those near you.
Whatever you lack, God has carefully stored in
someone near you. When your Enemy comes he often
exhausts your strength, your creativity and your
ideas. This usually launches your search to find the
Heavenly *treasure* God has stored in *earthen* vessels
near you. Remember—love is the secret code map
to the treasure!

54. Your Enemy Unifies Your Friends.
When the newspapers attacked me, I heard from
some lawyers and partners who I did not really know
even cared! Some wanted to sue, offering their legal
services for free!

55. The Holy Spirit Will Often Bring Conviction On Your Enemies.
"Who will have all
men to be saved, and to come unto the knowledge of
the truth," (1 Timothy 2:4). The jailor of Paul
experienced this. "Then he called for a light, and
sprang in, and came trembling, and fell down before
Paul and Silas, And brought them out, and said, Sirs,
what must I do to be saved?" (Acts 16:29-30).

"The Lord is not slack concerning His promise,
as some men count slackness; but is longsuffering to
us-ward, not willing that any should perish, but that
all should come to repentance," (2 Peter 3:9). Before
he became the Apostle Paul, Saul was an Enemy to
the church. But, God turned his heart. He can do
the same with your Enemy.

56. Your Enemy Today Could Possibly

Become Your Greatest Ally Tomorrow. It happened when the *tormentor* of the early church (Saul) became the *mentor* of the early church. "Then Ananias answered, Lord, I have heard by many of this man, how much evil he hath done to Thy saints at Jerusalem:...But the Lord said unto him, Go thy way: for he is a chosen vessel unto Me, to bear My name before the Gentiles, and kings, and the children of Israel," (Acts 9:13, 15).

57. Your Enemy May Be Suddenly And Dramatically Confronted By The Holy Spirit. He did it to Saul, before he became Paul. "And as he journeyed, he came near Damascus: and suddenly there shined round about him a light from Heaven: And he fell to the earth, and heard a voice saying unto him, Saul, Saul, why persecutest thou Me? And he said, Who art Thou, Lord? And the Lord said, I am Jesus whom thou persecutest: it is hard for thee to kick against the pricks," (Acts 9:3-5).

58. Your Enemy Can Experience A Sudden Change Of Heart. Saul became Paul...quickly. "And he trembling and astonished said, Lord, what wilt Thou have me to do? And the Lord said unto him, Arise, and go into the city, and it shall be told thee what thou must do," (Acts 9:6).

59. Your Enemy Can Completely Turn Around Because Of One Tragedy Or Crisis. "And Saul arose from the earth; and when his eyes were opened, he saw no man: but they led him by the hand, and brought him into Damascus. And he was three days without sight, and neither did eat nor drink," (Acts 9:8-9).

60. Your Enemy Is A Door, Not A Wall, To

Your Next Season. It happened for Esther. It happened for Daniel. It happened for Job. "The Lord gave Job twice as much as he had before," (Job 42:10).

61. The Only True Difference Between A Nobody And A Somebody Is The Enemy They Decided To Conquer. David went from a nobody to a Somebody...*through* Goliath. "And it came to pass as they came, when David was returned from the slaughter of the Philistine, that the women came out of all cities of Israel, singing and dancing to meet king Saul, with tabrets, with joy, and with instruments of music. And the women answered one another as they played, and said, Saul hath slain his thousands, and David his ten thousands," (1 Samuel 18:6-7).

62. Your Enemy Is The Difference Between Obscurity And Significance. Heavyweight champions have gone from unknown to world champions...in a single fight. When Evander Holyfield sees Mike Tyson walk through the door, he doesn't grab his ear! He grabs his checkbook! No friend of Evander Holyfield has ever given him $22 million...*It took an Enemy!* It happened to David (see 1 Samuel 18:6-7). Even bronco riders desire a mean bull so the judges can accurately assess their skills!

63. The Size Of Your Enemy Will Determine The Size Of Your Rewards. "And there went out a champion out of the camp of the Philistines, named Goliath, of Gath, whose height was six cubits and a span. And he had a helmet of brass upon his head, and he was armed with a coat of mail; and the weight of the coat was five thousand shekels of brass. And he had greaves of brass upon his legs, and a target of brass between his shoulders. And the staff of his spear was like a weaver's beam; and his spear's head weighed six hundred shekels of iron: and one bearing a shield went before him...And the men of Israel said, Have ye seen this man that is come up? surely to defy Israel is he come up: and it shall be, that the man who killeth him, the king will enrich him with great riches, and will give him his daughter, and make his father's house free in Israel," (1 Samuel 17:4-7, 25).

64. Your Enemy Forces Any Judas In Your Life To Reveal Himself. Judas is not your Enemy. Everybody has a Judas. Even Judases! Judases are *intimidated* by you. They work *undercover.* They betray you *behind your back.* A Judas is weak, spineless and intimidated. It is possible to live around a Judas for years and never discern it. They will not confront you. They attempt to weaken your influence with others through their words, their actions and conduct.

A Judas resents the love and loyalty expressed by others toward you.

A Judas is someone who believes your Enemy has a right to be heard. A Judas plays both parts: in *your* presence, a friend. In *their* presence, a friend.

When your Enemy enters, he will bond with the Judas in your Circle of Confidantes. Your Judas will be exposed quickly when an Enemy links with him.

Do not fear—when Judas is revealed, you are only *three days* from the *resurrection* of your whole life and future.

65. Anything Good Always Has An Enemy. *Evil* despises righteousness.

Fear despises faith.

Weakness despises strength.

Jesus was the very Son of God—yet the religious crowd despised Him.

66. You Will Only Be Remembered For The Enemy You Destroy Or The One Who Destroys You. Samson is remembered because Delilah deceived him. David is remembered for the Goliath he killed.

67. Your Enemy Can Not Abort Your Future— He Is Merely The Announcement That Your Future Is Being Born. When Goliath roared, David was receiving the announcement that his shepherd days were concluding. Kingship was being born.

68. Your Enemy Is As Necessary As Your Friend. Your friend gives you *comfort,* but your Enemy gives you a *future.*

69. Your Enemy Is Your Opportunity To Reveal Your Difference From Others. The brothers of David were angry, fearful and intimidated. *Nobody* would have discerned the *difference* in David...without Goliath. Your Enemy is an opportunity to reveal what you truly believe.

70. When You Discover Your Assignment, You Will Discover Your Enemy. Demonic warfare is a clue that satan has discovered the intentions of God toward you. Demons are *not* omnipresent. They cannot be everywhere simultaneously. They receive *geographical* assignments. This is apparent when the angel, answering the prayers of Daniel, mentions the warfare and the attempted interception of the message. He indicated that God had heard Daniel when he prayed. He was released and dispatched from Heaven. But, it took him 21 days to arrive.

"Then said he unto me, Fear not, Daniel: for from the first day that thou didst set thine heart to understand, and to chasten thyself before thy God, thy words were heard, and I am come from thy words. But the prince of the kingdom of Persia withstood me one and twenty days: but, lo, Michael, one of the chief princes, came to help me; and I remained there with the kings of Persia," (Daniel 10:12-13).

Where do we assign a security guard? Fifty miles from a bank vault? Of course not. He is assigned *where the treasure is located*. So, when you feel demonic activity around you, get excited. Satan is anticipating a miracle package arriving at your house. Warfare is his attempt to break your focus and abort your interest in the miracle.

71. The Favorite Entry Point Used By Your Enemy Will Usually Be Through Someone You Have Chosen To Trust. Your future depends on the weakness of the person you trust. Everybody trusts somebody. And, that person you are trusting is usually trusting someone you would not dream of trusting! Adam trusted Eve who opened the door to the serpent. Samson trusted Delilah. Your Enemy will always use someone you have chosen to trust.

72. The Enemy You Fail To Destroy Will Eventually Destroy You. The Prophet Samuel instructed Saul to kill the Amalekites utterly. He refused. He left king Agag alive with the best of the sheep and so forth. So, at Saul's death, the man who accepted the credit for finishing the suicidal attempt of Saul cried, "I am an Amalekite," (2 Samuel 1:9-10). What You Refuse To Conquer Will Eventually Conquer You.

73. You Will Never Outgrow Your Enemy— You Must Simply Learn To Fight. Many youth think that someday they will simply outgrow their desire to sin. Yet, the desire to sin is forever available. You must simply learn to fight back.

74. Struggle Is The Proof That You Have Not Yet Been Conquered By Your Enemy. You may be tired of fighting. Battle may weary you, but struggle is still the proof that your Enemy has not yet won.

75. Your Enemy Must Be Destroyed, Not Understood. Conversation is often the Door to Annihilation. It happened in the Garden of Eden. Satan moved Eve to the negotiation table to prepare them for alienation. Negotiate with *friends,* but *destroy* your Enemy.

76. Your Enemy Will Not Seek To Understand You, But To Discredit You. When I received bad press, they requested that I answer questions. I was happy to do so, but I requested their written verification that my entire answers would be printed...under the question asked.

They refused.

77. When God Completes A Season In Your Life, He Hardens The Heart Of An Enemy Toward You. Pharaoh's heart was hardened toward the Israelites. Why? It softened their heart about the move that God desired. In my little town here in Texas, I experienced the most incredible movements against the ministry. During my first partner meeting, police began to tow cars away during the service...though the little building we bought had been a Baptist church for over 30 years. Parking spaces had been used for years. But, God *hardened* their heart...to move our ministry to another location.

What you think is an Enemy trying to stop you is God's way of "boot kicking you" into the next season of your life.

78. Your Enemy Causes Good People To Find You. Many times, ministers have become unnoticed and unrecognized. But, during a season of attack, people who discerned truth became aware of them and bonded with them.

Bad Times Always Bring Good People Together.

79. Your Enemy Causes Unused And Dormant Gifts To Emerge. Adversity will expose hidden greatness within you. The brothers of David were totally blind to his *difference* from them.

80. Any Uncontested Enemy Will Flourish. Ignoring an Enemy does not remove him. Hoping your Enemy will leave does not remove him. You must contest your Enemy. "Resist the devil, and he will flee from you," (James 4:7).

81. Your Enemy Will Often Vary The Weapons And Strategy He Uses Against You. What he uses when you are a teenager may be completely different than what he uses when you are older.

82. The Reaction Of Your Enemy Is Proof Of Your Progress. When your Enemy gets anxious, he knows his time is limited.

83. Any Move You Make In The Right Direction Will Be Instantly Addressed By Your Enemy.

84. Your Enemy Will Ultimately Reveal The Greatness Of God To You. Your heart may doubt. Your mind may be confused. But, in a crisis, God will expose His power and love toward you. An

Enemy gives Him an opportunity to do so.

85. Your Enemy May Enter Your Life Under The Disguise Of Friendship. An Enemy may enter silently, quietly and begin to weaken your life like termites in a building. One evening, some years ago, my manager informed me that a young man had been sitting for hours in the staff sanctuary. He insisted on an appointment. I explained to her that he needed to schedule through my secretary. He replied to her that he had driven several hundred miles and wanted more than anything in the world to "just be the Protegé of Dr. Murdock...whatever it takes." He came in crying, weeping and begging for an opportunity to be an "armorbearer." Within weeks, he had started a slander campaign against me on my own staff. It was shocking. But, he had *entered* sweetly and quietly as a friend.

86. An Enemy Will Often Ignore Protocol And The Established Chain Of Authority. Rebellion is at the heart of an Enemy. He despises the *order* of God. I mentioned earlier about the young man who had wanted an appointment. He refused to accept the counsel of my manager to schedule with me the next day. I misread his aggressiveness.

Aggressiveness is not always proof of desire.

Aggressiveness is often rebellion to protocol.

My manager informed him that I could not see him that day. He replied, "I am determined to see him."

Later he cried to me, "You are what I have wanted to be around my entire life. I want you to become my Mentor. I will do anything to become your Protegé. Nobody has ever given me a chance.

Just give me a chance. I believe in you." Within weeks, he sowed more discord and strife into my staff than anyone in the history of my ministry.

He ignored *protocol*.

I ignored the *signal*.

87. Your Enemy Must Be Exposed. When there is a liar in your circle, expose them. You owe that to those under your protection. That's why Peter exposed Ananias and Sapphira (Acts 5:1-11).

You are responsible for any person you destroy.

You are also responsible for any person you *permit* to be destroyed.

One young staff member affected by another disgruntled staff member became a complete emotional wreck. She eventually left our ministry. She had been so loyal, so sweet and loving toward the things of God. Within days, he had confused her and left her shattered.

88. Your Enemy Will Attempt To Involve You In Unnecessary Battles Which Promise Little Or No Reward. Battles drain your energy. They break your focus and empty your resources.

89. Your Enemy Should Be Confronted In The Timing Of The Spirit And With The Right Spiritual Weaponry. This enables you to predict his strategy and conduct. The motivation of Peter to protect Jesus by cutting off the ear of the soldier is admirable, but it was not Spirit-led.

90. An Uncommon Enemy Can Be Defeated Through Uncommon Endurance. God requires endurance. "And ye shall be hated of all men for My name's sake: but he that endureth to the end shall be saved," (Matthew 10:22).

91. It Is Wisdom To Avoid Confrontation With Your Enemy When Possible. Jesus did this. "But when they persecute you in this city, flee ye into another," (Matthew 10:23). Fleeing does not demonstrate fear, but Wisdom to sustain your life and ministry and retain your focus.

92. It Is Wise To Make Peace With Your Enemy When Possible. "But I say unto you, That ye resist not evil: but whosoever shall smite thee on thy right cheek, turn to him the other also. And if any man will sue thee at the law, and take away thy coat, let him have thy cloke also. And whosoever shall compel thee to go a mile, go with him twain. Give to him that asketh thee, and from him that would borrow of thee turn not thou away," (Matthew 5:39-42).

Never use a tank to kill a mosquito.

Enemies are Bridges, not barricades.

Recognition Of The Enemy God Uses To Promote You Can Prevent Destruction, Protect Your Life And Those You Love.

❧ 20 ❧

RECOGNITION OF A FOOL

➤➣◦◄

The Wise Recognize Fools.

Fools are everywhere. There are fools in the educational institution, in the world of religion, in the political arena and even among your relatives.

Fools break your focus.

Fools waste valuable time and energy.

Fools slow your life down.

Fools rob you of precious moments.

I mentioned a statement by former President Richard Nixon in one of my books, *Secrets of the Richest Man Who Ever Lived.* He commented that Lee Iacoca, the legendary leader of Chrysler, had one major problem—no tolerance for fools. Nixon further explained that his attitude created two more problems! First, there are so many fools and second, some people that you think are fools really are not!

43 Important Facts You Should Know About Fools

1. A Fool Is Anyone Who Despises Wisdom, Instruction And Correction From A Proven Mentor. "The fear of the Lord is the beginning of knowledge: but fools despise wisdom and instruction," (Proverbs 1:7).

2. A Fool Is Anyone Who Attempts To

Destroy The Reputation Of A Proven Champion Through Lying And Misrepresentation. "He that uttereth a slander, is a fool," (Proverbs 10:18).

3. **A Fool Is Anyone Who Refuses To Depart From Evil, Even Though Corrected.** "But it is abomination to fools to depart from evil," (Proverbs 13:19).

4. **A Fool Is Anyone Who Does Not Take The Danger Of Sin Seriously.** "Fools make a mock at sin: but among the righteous there is favour," (Proverbs 14:9).

5. **A Fool Is Anyone Who Reveals Confidences That Should Be Kept Private.** "Wisdom resteth in the heart of him that hath understanding: but that which is in the midst of fools is made known," (Proverbs 14:33).

6. **A Fool Is Any Son That Disregards The Wisdom Of His Father.** "A fool despiseth his father's instruction: but he that regardeth reproof is prudent," (Proverbs 15:5).

7. **A Fool Is Any Son Who Shows Disrespect Toward The Mother That Brought Him Into The World.** "A wise son maketh a glad father: but a foolish man despiseth his mother," (Proverbs 15:20).

8. **A Fool Is Anyone Whose Conduct Does Not Change Even After Experiencing Painful Consequences From It.** "A reproof entereth more into a wise man than an hundred stripes into a fool," (Proverbs 17:10).

9. **A Fool Is Anyone Who Considers Any Pursuit Of Wisdom To Be A Wasted Effort.** "Wherefore is there a price in the hand of a fool to

get wisdom, seeing he hath no heart to it?" (Proverbs 17:16).

10. A Fool Is Anyone Who Continually Expresses His Discontent With God. "The foolishness of man perverteth his way: and his heart fretteth against the Lord," (Proverbs 19:3).

11. A Fool Is Anyone Who Refuses To Embrace Peace. "It is an honour for a man to cease from strife: but every fool will be meddling," (Proverbs 20:3).

12. A Fool Is Any Man Who Spends More Money Than He Is Willing To Earn For His Family. "There is treasure to be desired and oil in the dwelling of the wise; but a foolish man spendeth it up," (Proverbs 21:20).

13. A Fool Is Anyone Who Creates His Own Belief System, Contrary To The Word Of God. "He that trusteth in his own heart is a fool: but whoso walketh wisely, he shall be delivered," (Proverbs 28:26).

14. A Fool Is Anyone Who Refuses To Pay His Debts. "When thou vowest a vow unto God, defer not to pay it; for He hath no pleasure in fools: pay that which thou hast vowed. Better is it that thou shouldest not vow, than that thou shouldest vow and not pay," (Ecclesiastes 5:4-5).

15. A Fool Is Anyone Who Makes Financial Increase His Life Focus Rather Than God. "But God said unto him, Thou fool, this night thy soul shall be required of thee: then whose shall those things be, which thou hast provided? So is he that layeth up treasure for himself, and is not rich toward God," (Luke 12:20-21).

16. A Fool Is Someone Who Wants

Something He Has Not Yet Earned. Ahab's wife, Queen Jezebel, was also a fool. Her husband's bitter words concerning the man with the vineyard angered her heart. Why? She wanted something she had not yet earned.

17. A Fool That Keeps Silent Often Remains Undetected. "Even a fool, when he holdeth his peace, is counted wise: and he that shutteth his lips is esteemed a man of understanding," (Proverbs 17:28).

18. A Fool Is Always At The Center Of Strife And Contention. "A fool's lips enter into contention, and his mouth calleth for strokes. A fool's mouth is his destruction, and his lips are the snare of his soul," (Proverbs 18:6-7).

19. Any Companion To Fools Will Ultimately Be Destroyed. "He that walketh with wise men shall be wise: but a companion of fools shall be destroyed," (Proverbs 13:20).

20. The Wise Always Leave The Presence Of Fools When They Perceive A Lack Of Desire For Knowledge. "Go from the presence of a foolish man, when thou perceivest not in him the lips of knowledge," (Proverbs 14:7).

21. Liars Are Fools. "He that hideth hatred with lying lips...is a fool," (Proverbs 10:18). A liar destroys his trustworthiness with a single sentence. He will trade a lifetime relationship for a single falsehood. Without a doubt, he is a fool.

22. A Fool Is Usually Only Changed By Correction During His Childhood. "Foolishness is bound in the heart of a child; but the rod of correction shall drive it far from him," (Proverbs 22:15).

23. A Fool Cannot Be Changed Through Counsel. "Speak not in the ears of a fool: for he will despise the wisdom of thy words," (Proverbs 23:9).

24. A Fool Should Never Be Given A Position Of Leadership Over Others. "Wisdom is too high for a fool: he openeth not his mouth in the gate," (Proverbs 24:7). In the ancient days, the wise elders of the city met at the gates of the city. Fools were never welcomed or given position of influence there.

25. The Continuous Threat Of Pain Is The Only Influence That Keeps A Fool In His Place. "A whip for the horse, a bridle for the ass, and a rod for the fool's back," (Proverbs 26:3).

26. A Fool Who Is Trusted Ultimately Destroys Those Who Trusted Him. "He that sendeth a message by the hand of a fool cutteth off the feet, and drinketh damage," (Proverbs 26:6).

27. A Fool Remains Unaffected Or Changed By Any Wisdom He Quotes From Others. "The legs of the lame are not equal: so is a parable in the mouth of fools," (Proverbs 26:7).

28. A Fool, When Given A Position Of Honor Or Power, Becomes Deadly To Those Within His Influence. "As he that bindeth a stone in a sling, so is he that giveth honour to a fool," (Proverbs 26:8).

29. Every Fool Will Eventually Taste The Consequences Of His Attitude And Rebellion. "The great God that formed all things both rewardeth the fool, and rewardeth transgressors," (Proverbs 26:10).

30. A Fool Is Someone Who Makes The Same Mistakes Repeatedly. "As a dog returneth to his vomit, so a fool returneth to his folly," (Proverbs 26:11).

31. A Fool Uses His Anger To Threaten To Create Problems For Others. "A stone is heavy, and the sand weighty; but a fool's wrath is heavier than them both," (Proverbs 27:3).

32. A Fool Exposed Is More Destructive Than Wild Animals Disturbed. "Let a bear robbed of her whelps meet a man, rather than a fool in his folly," (Proverbs 17:12).

33. No Amount Of Wisdom Or Counsel Can Create A Peaceful Relationship With A Fool. "If a wise man contendeth with a foolish man, whether he rage or laugh, there is no rest," (Proverbs 29:9).

34. A Fool Tells Everything He Knows And Feels To Others. "A fool uttereth all his mind: but a wise man keepeth it in till afterwards," (Proverbs 29:11).

35. A Fool Talks Too Much And Is Known By His Torrent Of Words. "A fool also is full of words: a man cannot tell what shall be; and what shall be after him, who can tell him?" (Ecclesiastes 10:14). "A fool's voice is known by multitude of words," (Ecclesiastes 5:3).

36. A Fool Never Believes That He Is Wrong. "Keep thy foot when thou goest to the house of God, and be more ready to hear, than to give the sacrifice of fools: for they consider not that they do evil," (Ecclesiastes 5:1).

37. The Parents Of A Fool Will Live In Sorrow Their Entire Lifetime. "He that begetteth a fool doeth it to his sorrow: and the father of a fool hath no joy," (Proverbs 17:21). "A foolish son is a grief to his father, and bitterness to her that bare him," (Proverbs 17:25).

38. Any Atheist Is A Fool. "The fool hath said in his heart, There is no God," (Psalm 14:1; see also Psalm 53:1).

39. A Fool Does Not Learn From His Observation Nor Experiences Enough To Make Changes. "Wisdom is before him that hath understanding; but the eyes of a fool are in the ends of the earth," (Proverbs 17:24).

40. Any Conversation With Fools Should Be Avoided. Association is defiling. Correction is useless. Solomon understood this. "Answer not a fool according to his folly, lest thou also be like unto him," (Proverbs 26:4). He refused to enter into any relationship or conversation.

41. A Fool Perpetuates His Offenses To Others Around Him. He wants others to feel his pain. He arouses an army of protesters against someone who offended him, rather than exhibiting a desire to settle the offense.

42. A Fool Refuses To Admit His Mistakes Even When His Pain Is The Obvious Result.

43. A Fool Refuses To Reach For Counsel From Accessible Champions. When I heard several complaints over financial problems, I offered to pay the registration to "The Uncommon Millionaire's Conference." I brought in six multi-millionaires to advise on financial blessing for three days. Those who had been complaining of their finances...*never even attended* the 21 hours of teaching at the conference, though some lived less than 5 minutes away.

Recognition Of A Fool Will Enable You To Avoid A Thousand Heartbreaking Experiences In Your Life.

"Moreover as for me, God forbid that I
should sin against the Lord in ceasing
to pray for you."
1 Samuel 12:23

❧ 21 ❧

RECOGNITION OF AN INTERCESSOR ASSIGNED TO YOU

━━━━━➤-◦-◄━━━━━

Prayer Is The Greatest Weapon Of Your Life.
Lost battles are evidences that The Weapon was *unused.*

18 Facts You Should Know About Intercessory Prayer

1.   God Commanded Us To Pray. "Men ought always to pray, and not to faint," (Luke 18:1).

2. ˙ **Prayer Pleasures The Heart Of God.** "And there I will meet with thee, and I will commune with thee from above the mercy seat, from between the two cherubims which are upon the ark of the testimony, of all things which I will give thee in commandment unto the children of Israel," (Exodus 25:22).

3.   Prayer Will Pleasure Your Own Spirit. "Come unto Me, all ye that labour and are heavy laden, and I will give you rest," (Matthew 11:28).

4.   Prayer Affects The Lives Of Others. "I exhort therefore, that, first of all, supplications, prayers, intercessions, and giving of thanks, be made for all men," (1 Timothy 2:1).

5.   Prayer Births Uncommon Miracles.

"Call unto Me, and I will answer thee, and shew thee great and mighty things, which thou knowest not," (Jeremiah 33:3).

6. Your Prayer Requests Should Be Made Directly To The Father. "And in that day ye shall ask Me nothing. Verily, verily, I say unto you, Whatsoever ye shall ask the Father in My name, He will give it you," (John 16:23).

7. Every Prayer Request Should Be Made In The Name Of Jesus. "Whatsoever ye shall ask in My name, that will I do, that the Father may be glorified in the Son. If ye shall ask any thing in My name, I will do it. If ye love Me, keep My commandments," (John 14:13-15).

8. Prayer Reveals Humility. It reveals confidence and faith in God. It is the proof of your respect for God.

9. Intercessors Are Those Called To Pray For You. As Samuel said, "Moreover as for me, God forbid that I should sin against the Lord in ceasing to pray for you," (1 Samuel 12:23).

10. Intercession Was The Habit Of Jesus. "And it came to pass in those days, that He went out into a mountain to pray, and continued all night in prayer to God," (Luke 6:12).

11. Intercessors Are Sought Out By God. "And I sought for a man among them, that should make up the hedge, and stand in the gap before Me for the land, that I should not destroy it: but I found none," (Ezekiel 22:30).

12. Intercessors Are Needed By Every One Of Us. Peter needed intercessors. While he was in prison, others interceded for him. "Peter therefore was kept in prison: but prayer was made without ceasing of the church unto God for him," (Acts 12:5).

God sent an angel, released him from prison, *because of Intercessors.*

13. Intercession Is The Habit Of Uncommon Champions Of God. The Apostle Paul was brilliant. He knew Scripture. He knew the art of persuasion. But, he also understood the incredible force that his prayers had. He wrote to Timothy, "I thank God, whom I serve from my forefathers with pure conscience, that without ceasing I have remembrance of thee in my prayers night and day," (2 Timothy 1:3).

14. Intercession Is Occurring Right Now In Heaven For You. Jesus is your Intercessor. "It is Christ that died, yea rather, that is risen again, Who is even at the right hand of God, Who also maketh intercession for us," (Romans 8:34).

15. Intercession Occurs Daily For You By The Holy Spirit Within You. "Likewise the Spirit also helpeth our infirmities: for we know not what we should pray for as we ought: but the Spirit [Himself] maketh intercession for us with groanings which cannot be uttered. And He that searcheth the hearts knoweth what is the mind of the Spirit, because He maketh intercession for the saints according to the will of God," (Romans 8:26-27).

16. The Intercession Of Jesus Protected Peter From Spiritual Destruction. "And the Lord said, Simon, Simon, behold, satan hath desired to have you, that he may sift you as wheat: But I have prayed for thee, that thy faith fail not: and when thou art converted, strengthen thy brethren," (Luke 22:31-32). Peter would not fail, because of the intercession of Jesus for him. Jesus expected His prayers to produce results.

17. Intercessors Prevent Tragedies From

Occurring In Our Lives. Lot experienced this. When the sin of Sodom and Gomorrah infuriated God, He came down to destroy those two wicked cities. Lot, his wife and family lived in those cities. Abraham interceded to God on behalf of them. The mercies of God were released. Lot and his two daughters escaped...*because of the prayers of Abraham* on behalf of that city. "And it came to pass, when God destroyed the cities of the plain, that God remembered Abraham, and sent Lot out of the midst of the overthrow, when He overthrew the cities in the which Lot dwelt," (Genesis 19:29). It was not the goodness of Lot that created his deliverance. It was the memory of God regarding Abraham's intercession.

18. When You Recognize The Intercessors God Has Assigned To Your Life, Your Respect For Them Will Bring Great Results. Every month, I send thousands of Faith Agreement Pages to my friends and partners. Some simply throw them away. However, many rush those Faith Agreement Pages back to me...and write me later about the incredible results.

When You Respect Your Intercessors, Your Life Will Experience The Greatest Parade Of Miracles You Ever Dreamed Possible.

RECOMMENDED BOOKS AND TAPES ON THIS TOPIC

B-07   Battle Techniques for War-Weary Saints (32 pages/$5)
B-14   Seeds of Wisdom on Relationships (32 pages/$3)
B-23   Seeds of Wisdom on Prayer (32 pages/$3)
B-27   The Jesus Book (166 pages/$10)
B-56   How to Turn Your Mistakes into Miracles (32 pages/$5)
B-69   Wisdom Keys for a Powerful Prayer Life (32 pages/$3)
B-100 The Holy Spirit Handbook, Vol. 1 (153 pages/$10)
B-115 Seeds of Wisdom on The Secret Place (32 pages/$5)
TS-08 The Strategy of Hourly Obedience (6 tapes/$30)
TS-29 The Holy Spirit Handbook (6 tapes/$30)

◦ 22 ◦

RECOGNITION OF THE SEED GOD HAS GIVEN YOU TO SOW

━━━►›◦‹◄━━━

You Will Reap What You Sow.
Scriptures prove it. "Be not deceived; God is not mocked: for whatsoever a man soweth, that shall he also reap," (Galatians 6:7).

21 Facts You Should Know About Seed-Faith

1. Your Seed Is Anything You Have Received From God That You Can Sow Into Someone Else.
Thoughts are Seeds.
Love is a Seed.
Time is a Seed.
Patience is a Seed.
Mercy is a Seed.
Kindness is a Seed.
Money is a Seed.
Your *Prayers* are Seeds.
Thankfulness is a Seed.
2. Seed-Faith Is Sowing What You Have Been Given To Create Something Else You Have Been Promised.

3. Your Seed Is The Tool God Has Given You To Create Your Future. Look at David. He complained about the armor of Saul. But, he had another tool—the slingshot. It was simple. Overlooked. Ignored by other soldiers. It was The *Seed* that God had placed in his hand. It was his supernatural tool! God always leaves you with *something*. What is it? *Find it.*

4. Something You Have Been Given By God Will Create Anything Else You Have Ever Been Promised By God. Tenacity in the woman who hemorrhaged for twelve years, created the miracle of touching the hem of Jesus' garment. The loaves and fishes of a small lad created enough for the multitude. Stop looking at what others possess. Instead, start thanking God for something He has already given you.

5. There Will Never Be A Day In Your Life That You Have Nothing. You may be impoverished like the widow. Many think she had nothing. She had something—powerful, incredible and rare.

She had the ability to *discern* a man of God.

She had the ability to *listen* to a man of God.

She had the ability to *obey* a man of God.

6. God Always Gives You Something To Begin Your Future. David had a *slingshot* to create a victory. The widow had a *meal* to invest into a man of God. You have *something!* Look for it again!

7. You Are A Walking Warehouse Of Remarkable Seeds. Most people have no idea what they contain! They waste thousands of hours studying their losses instead of taking inventory of what they have been given. They look at what they have *not* instead of what they have *got*.

Listen carefully. It is rarely destructive or devastating to take an inventory of all the things you need and desire. But it is tragic beyond words if you fail to *recognize your Seeds*—what you have received from God to plant into the lives of others. Stop focusing on losses. Look longer, closer and thankfully at something you have *already* been given and presently have.

8. Something You Already Possess Is Your Key To Your Future. It may be knowledge, money, skills or ideas, insights and concepts. You *already* have enough to create your future.

9. Everything You Have Was Given To You By God. Don't become cocky over tithing your small amount of ten percent. Your *entire* paycheck came from God! Your *eyesight* came from God! Your *hearing* came from God! Your *health* came from God! Your *intelligence* came from God! Your *Favor* from others came from God! You don't have a thing that God did not give you.

10. If You Keep What You Presently Have, That Is The Most It Will Ever Be. When you sow it, it is the least it will ever be. This is one of the most vital principles you must understand in unleashing an *Uncommon Harvest.* Releasing what you have is the only evidence of your faith that God will provide for you.

11. A Seed Of Nothing Guarantees A Season Of Nothing. Years ago, The Holy Spirit spoke to me to plant a beautiful Mercedes into the life of another. I was upset with this person. I refused. I have wondered about the Harvest I lost...many times. If a Seed of *Something* can create *Something,* it is quite obvious—a Seed of *Nothing* will create a Season of *Nothing* in your life.

12. Your Seed Sowing Is The Only Proof You Have Mastered Greed. Men hoard. Satan steals. God has the nature of giving. Giving Is The Only Cure For Greed. Your Seed is the proof that you have mastered hoarding, selfishness and greed.

13. When You Let Go Of What Is In Your Hand, God Will Let Go Of What Is In His Hand. When the small lad released the loaves and fishes into the hands of Jesus, the multiplication began. They picked up several baskets later!

14. Every Seed Contains An Invisible Instruction. You cannot see it. It is invisible. Yet, a small watermelon seed will follow that instruction and produce more watermelons. The tomato seed will create more tomatoes. Each Seed contains a specific Assignment. The Creator placed it inside.

15. When You Give Your Seed A Specific Assignment, Faith And Expectation Are Unleashed. The widow was demoralized. But, the man of God gave her a Portrait of Possibility. She was encouraged to plant a Seed so she would not lack. She did. Faith was born. "And she went and did according to the saying of Elijah: and she, and he, and her house, did eat many days," (1 Kings 17:15).

16. When You Increase The Size Of

Your Seed, You Increase The Size Of Your Harvest. "But this I say, he which soweth sparingly shall reap also sparingly; and he which soweth bountifully shall reap also bountifully," (2 Corinthians 9:6).

17. When You Get Involved With God's Dream, He Will Get Involved With Your Dream. That's the power of sowing. You create a Covenant. Think of a tiny Seed that enters into a Covenant with the soil. Within weeks, it has cracked a concrete slab!! That's the Power of Two...The Covenant. The widow invested into Elijah. God, then, entered into a Covenant with her that she would never lack in the famine (read 1 Kings 17).

18. You Can Only Sow What You Have Been Given. Stop complaining about something you do not have. You lack money? Then, use your Time as a Seed. Work for your boss, the local church or simply baby-sit for someone overworked! Use your Time as a Seed.

19. Your Seed Is Always Your Door Out Of Trouble. It was for the widow. It can be for you. It may be information, motivation or encouragement. Give it an Assignment. It can produce an exit from your present season.

20. When God Talks To You About A Seed, He Has A Harvest On His Mind.

21. An Uncommon Seed Always Creates An Uncommon Harvest. An Uncommon Seed is one that requires uncommon faith...or, a Seed you sow during a season of uncommon hardship.

Here is one of my miracles I shared in my book, *7 Keys to 1000 Times More.*

How I Broke The Back Of Poverty
In My Life!

I *broke the back of poverty* with an Uncommon Seed. A Seed of $1,000. I will never forget it as long as I live. It happened on a telethon. I had just received an incredible royalty check for my song writing of $5,000. I was ecstatic! You see, I didn't have anything. Sheets were tacked over my windows. I wanted draperies so bad. I needed a kitchen table with chairs. I had *nothing!* So, I really had wonderful plans for my $5,000! It was my Harvest!

Suddenly, The Holy Spirit spoke to me while sitting next to some ministers on the telethon.

"I want you to plant a Seed of $1,000."

Well, I explained to The Holy Spirit, that I was going to buy draperies and a kitchen table with chairs! (It took me over 45 minutes before I fully obeyed Him.)

The next day, He spoke again. I planted a *second* Seed of $1,000. Then the following Sunday morning, The Holy Spirit spoke to me the *third* time to plant a *third* Seed of $1,000 at a church in Dallas. That afternoon cannot be explained or described adequately! I was in torment and ecstasy at the same time. I felt a little sick inside because I felt like I had gotten "carried away." I knelt at the pastor's little office that afternoon before service. My heart was quite troubled.

"Holy Spirit, five days ago I had $5,000. Within the last five days, You have spoken to me to plant three Seeds of $1,000. If this is not You and Your plan, stop me now!"

The Holy Spirit gently conveyed that *when*

He talked to me about a Seed, He had a Harvest on His mind. When I opened my hand, He would open His windows. The Seed that would leave my hand would never leave my life—just my hand, and enter into my future where it would multiply!

The miracles began.

That night, a man approached me. He opened a book featuring rare automobiles. He explained one of the cars in it. "There's only 19 of these in the world. I happen to have Serial Number 1— the first one they made. It is my pet car. *God told me to give it to you!*"

The *next* day, a man walked into my office. He said, "I understand you need a van for your ministry. Order the best one you can buy. *I'll pay for it.*"

Tuesday morning, the next day, a friend met me for lunch. He explained that he could not sleep that night. The Holy Spirit told him to plant a special Seed of $10,000 into my ministry!

My life has never been the same.

Within a couple of years, over $300,000 came into my pocket and life from song-writing royalties. It was astounding.

Recognition Of Your Seed Can Unlock A Thousand Harvests You Thought Were Impossible.

RECOMMENDED BOOKS AND TAPES ON THIS TOPIC
B-04   Ten Lies Many People Believe About Money (32 pages/$5)
B-06   Creating Tomorrow Through Seed-Faith (32 pages/$5)
B-16   Seeds of Wisdom on Seed-Faith (32 pages/$3)
B-47   The Covenant of Fifty-Eight Blessings (82 pages/$8)
B-82   31 Reasons People Do Not Receive Their Financial Harvest (252 pages/ $12)
B-91   The Leadership Secrets of Jesus (196 pages/$10)
B-101   The 3 Most Important Things in Your Life (240 pages/$10)
B-104   7 Keys to 1000 Times More (128 pages/$10)
TS-62   31 Secrets to Financial Breakthrough (6 tapes/$30)

"Your Harvest Is Any Person, Provision, Idea, Opportunity Or Act Of Favor That Solves A Problem For You."
-MIKE MURDOCK

~ 23 ~

RECOGNITION OF A HARVEST GOD SENDS TO YOU

Harvests Occur Daily In Your Life.
Your Harvest Is Any Good Thing In Your Life.
▶ *Any Person* who blesses, encourages, corrects, strengthens or improves you.
▶ *Any Idea* planted by your Creator that has potential for helping others.
▶ *Any Opportunity* to increase your finances, maximize your standard of excellence or unlock a gift or skill within you. It is any opportunity you have to solve a problem.
Few recognize their Harvest when it occurs.

My father is a powerful Golden Harvest in my life. He has prayed six to ten hours every day that I can recall. He is 89 years old today, still full of passion for God. He is obsessed with Scripture. I have never heard him tell a lie, curse or say one sentence that could not be placed on the front page of a newspaper anywhere. He walks with God. My greatest and most familiar memory is him on his knees with his hands uplifted and praying in a Heavenly language.

He was a strong disciplinarian. His whippings

last in my memory in an unforgettable way. Yet, I never heard him raise his voice once in my lifetime. He never screamed. Mother never yelled at any of us. I am still saying, "Yes sir." And, "No sir." You see, he is a Harvest from God because he *warned, disciplined and kept me in the presence of God.*

Your Harvests Are Coming Toward You Every Moment Of Your Life. It is your responsibility to recognize them.

I have spoken at a trucking company banquet several times. Every Christmas, it has been my privilege to speak there. My last visit, a trucker came up, "Mike, you told us about planting that Seed of $58 the last time you were here, but nothing happened. It didn't work for me."

"You didn't get any Harvest *at all?*" I asked.

"Nope. Nothing."

He kept some small talk going while my mind raced for an appropriate question. You see, I think any man who could look God in the face and say that he has never received anything from the hand of God has a serious problem. (Wisdom may *not always* make you bold, but, *ignorance* always makes you bold.) We talked a while. In a few minutes, he stated, "You know, something crazy happened a few weeks ago. I was driving down this freeway over here, and my semi and trailer jack-knifed. Practically came off the freeway. Could have killed me. Luckily, I got out without a scratch. Crazy, isn't it?"

This is the same man who told me five minutes before, "It didn't work for me. I've never received a Harvest from my Seed."

Almost nobody recognizes a Harvest when it occurs. He could have been paralyzed from his neck down. A leg could have been chopped off. He could have died leaving his family without a provider. His *safety* was a Miracle Harvest, but *he never recognized it.*

Every night you are permitted the privilege of driving into your garage. Look up at that beautiful moon and stop and say, *"Thank you for another beautiful Harvest today, Father."*

You see, He kept His angels around you every moment of the day. You did not wake up in a hospital with tubes running from your body. Sir, listen to me.

That Is A Harvest.

Thousands never made it back home today, *but you did.* When you wake up in the morning breathing, alive and well, look out your window. *If you can see a sun rising in the morning,* beautiful and glowing, you have just received *another* Harvest. Thousands have never seen a sunrise *in their lifetime.*

When you sit down tonight at supper, look carefully at the bowls full of food. You can eat until you are stuffed and overflowing.

That Is A Harvest.

I can take you to parts of the world such as Calcutta, India, where children die every single night because they could not find enough crumbs in the trash to survive another day.

When you swallow your food and digest it, you have just received *another Harvest.* Thousands are in hospitals this very moment who cannot feed themselves.

When you drove in the traffic this morning, en route to a full day's work, you just received *another Harvest.* Millions would give anything today if they knew their *reason* to wake up. But, they are unemployed. They are looking for a place of significance.

That Is A Harvest.

Can you hear the incredible music coming across the wind, or from your stereo? Thousands cannot hear a sound. But, you have just received *another Harvest.* As you lay your head on your pillow tonight, stare at the ceiling a few moments. It may rain, but you will not be disturbed. The winds may blow hard, but you will not sense it. Lightning may flash, but you are safe. You have a shelter over your head.

That Is A Harvest.

When your child comes running up to you saying, "Daddy, Daddy," you throw your arms out and welcome that child. Yet, thousands of parents have lost their children. Disease, accidents, irreversible situations have created a great vacuum within them. Their house is silent, screaming with the loneliness. Many mothers would give anything in the world to hear their child cry in the middle of the night. The father would trade every penny in his savings account to see his little boy run across the yard *just one more time.* Yet, your own children are around you today.

That Is A Harvest.

As I awakened this morning, I swung my legs to the side of the bed. I sat there, then moved into the bathroom where I punched "play" on my cassette player. I began to hear the deep, powerful rich voice speaking the Scriptures aloud on the cassette. My heart begins to throb. His presence fills the room.

That Is A Harvest.

Millions are unsaved, unchanged and untaught. Yet, you have *learned*. You have *discovered*. You have *Jesus*. He has changed your life.

That Is A Harvest.

As you sit in your beautiful car today, air conditioned and safe, replay in your mind the thousands of refugees who are crawling across the desert tonight looking for a tent where they can take their family and drink a cup of water. A slice of bread is celebrated by them. They have lost their home due to the war and conflicts in their country. You will see it on the news every night of your life. Yet, you will pull up at a restaurant in a few hours, purchase a hamburger, and complain because something has been left off the sandwich. Perhaps the pickles or you received mustard instead of mayonnaise. You will find something to complain about. Oh, my friend, unthankfulness was the first sin, and God has not forgotten.

Your life has been a parade of Harvests.

You must learn to *recognize* your Harvest.

10 Facts About Your Harvest

1. Your Harvest Is Any Person Or Anything That Can Bless Or Benefit You. It may be someone who can contribute something you need— information, Favor, finances, an explosive idea or encouragement when you need it most.

2. Your Harvest Already Exists. It is walking around you! Just as your eyes had to be opened to recognize Jesus, your eyes also must be opened to *recognize your Harvests* as they come.

3. Access To Someone Who Believes In You Is A Harvest. Every Golden Connection is a

Harvest.

4. Your Harvest Occurs When Someone Recommends You To Others. Any flow of Favor and acceptance toward your life is a Harvest.

5. The Entire World Missed The Harvest Of Jesus. "He was in the world, and the world was made by Him, and the world knew Him not. He came unto His own, and His own received him not," (John 1:10-11). How tragic! Spiritual leaders, such as the Pharisees, failed to recognize Him! Politicians of His day *failed to see Him as their Harvest.*

6. Everything You Possess Came From Him.

7. Everything You Will Ever Own In Your Future Must Come From Him.

8. Your Miracle Harvest Is Going Past You Every Day. You may be failing to see it. Failing to appropriate it. Failing to be *thankful* for it.

9. You Must Stop What You Are Doing Long Enough To Celebrate The Good Happening Around You.

10. You Are Continuously Moving Toward A Glorious Harvest. Something marvelous is also moving toward you. Can you slow down long enough to discern it?

That is why I am baffled, bewildered and angered at the vicious, malicious, unexplainable attack on the message of sowing Seed for a Harvest.

Recently, I wept before a large group of ministers and cried out, *"Will somebody explain to me why The Offering Time is so painful for you?* Please tell me why you can spend two hours on Friday night sponsoring a basketball game for your teenagers, but you think fifteen minutes in a service discussing The

Seed and The Harvest is *too long?* Please explain that! Somebody tell me why it's permissible to sit for 90 minutes at a 24-hour restaurant for pancakes after church, but a 90 minute message on prosperity from the hand of the Multiplier and Provider aggravates, agitates and infuriates us? Please explain to me. Tell me why The Offering turns you off!"

"Somebody please tell me why it was all right for Jesus to die like a dog on Calvary; eight inches of thorns crushed into His brow; a spear in His side and spikes in His hands; 400 soldiers spitting on His body; 39 stripes tearing His back to shreds; His beard ripped off His face. Yet, talking about bringing a little dime out of each dollar back to the House of God infuriates those who claim to be in love with Him. Will somebody please explain that?"

What do you have that God did not give you? It is He that keeps breathing His breath into you.

You could not breathe another minute *if God did not breathe into you.*

You could not walk another step *if God were not there.*

You could not live another day *if His presence were withheld from you.*

I looked at hundreds of pastors in Washington, D.C., and cried out, "Please explain why you are embarrassed to celebrate sowing a Seed into the work of Jesus Christ! *Why? Why? Why?* Why is that so humiliating to you? Why are you so bold and audacious and brash enough to ask God for a continuous *stream of miracles* for everybody in your church, yet you don't have enough boldness to look in the face of your people and instruct them to bring

The Offering to the front and place it openly and joyfully in His hand? Why? Is it a reward for a boxer to receive $14 million dollars for 90 seconds of boxing? Another athlete receives $40 million dollars for bouncing a basketball. Yet, why is bringing 10 cents to God so burdensome to us?

Why is it painful for us to ask somebody to sow a Seed of $20 to exalt the name of Jesus, the greatest Name on earth that brings men out of hell into Heaven?"

Oh, listen to me! Hear my heart today! When your pastor receives an offering, he has just *opened the door for you to change the seasons of your life.*

You may whine about it.

You may complain about it.

You may sneer and ridicule.

You may even say idiotic things like, "I am so glad our pastor never talks about money." Frankly, I would never attend a church that didn't discuss money often. You see, I think about supply every day of my life. The last thing I need is someone who ignores the greatest needs in my life!

Some board members recently discussed the salary of their pastor with me. They were concerned. They felt his income might be a little larger than necessary.

"Is your family ready for Heaven should they die?" I asked. "Whose teaching has sustained them and kept them close to God?"

As we talked, their eyes widened. They understood. They were actually considering lowering his salary, yet their pastor was the *Prayer Covering* over their lives, *driving back the darkness of error, smashing the locks* on their mental prisons, and *bringing them into the presence of God* whose peace and joy was multiplied in their lives.

Their *pastor* had changed them forever.

Yet, they did not recognize him as their Harvest.

Discern your Harvest.

Nobody else can do it for you. Nobody.

Nobody else *should* do it for you.

You are responsible for your life, your Seed and *your Harvests.*

"Oh, I wish I could try one more time," a woman cried. "I made a huge mistake with my husband. It was my fault. He was the greatest man I ever knew, but I focused on his flaws. I want to go back home, but I can't." It was too late.

Her Harvest had been lost.

Often I hear, "Dr. Mike, I give and give and give, but God never gives it back to me. I never receive the Harvest. What should I do?"

That question haunts me. How could any person who had any discerning at all of the blessings of God stand boldly and unashamedly and say, "God never blesses me?" It's explainable. *That individual has no idea what a Harvest even looks like.*

Do you?

Oh, friend, recognize any ingratitude on your part and repent immediately.

Any Harvest unrecognized is uncelebrated. Any Harvest uncelebrated is a monument to unthankfulness.

Our prayer together...

"Father, forgive us for ingratitude, unthankfulness and *any blindness toward The Harvests* You have provided. It is true that our complaining spirit has robbed us and aborted many miracles You had scheduled for us. In the name of Jesus, I release myself to You. I give all of me to You, knowing that You will reveal wonderful and powerful things to me.

Thank You for my *health*, my *eyesight* and *ability to walk* today.

Thank You for the *mind* that You have given me, and the *doors of Favor* that have opened into my life. You are a marvelous, powerful and giving God.

I am thankful. I am grateful.

I shall not forget Your blessing on my life.

I'll be swift to give You the glory and praise for every good thing You do for me. You will receive the tithe of everything You give to me.

I *thank You* for every blessing. In the Name of Jesus. Amen."

Recognition Of Your Harvests Will Destroy The Root Of Bitterness, Unleash An Enthusiasm Unparalleled And Open A Thousand Doors Of Favor In Your Lifetime.

RECOMMENDED BOOKS AND TAPES ON THIS TOPIC

B-04   Ten Lies Many People Believe About Money (32 pages/$5)
B-06   Creating Tomorrow Through Seed-Faith (32 pages/$5)
B-16   Seeds of Wisdom on Seed-Faith (32 pages/$3)
B-47   The Covenant of Fifty-Eight Blessings (82 pages/$8)
B-82   31 Reasons People Do Not Receive Their Financial Harvest (252 pages/ $12)
B-101   The 3 Most Important Things in Your Life (240 pages/$10)
B-104   7 Keys to 1000 Times More (128 pages/$10)
TS-62   31 Secrets to Financial Breakthrough (6 tapes/$30)
TS-30   7 Keys to 1000 Times More (6 tapes/$30)
TS-38   31 Reasons People Do Not Receive Their Financial Harvest (6 tapes/ $30)

∾ 24 ∾

RECOGNITION OF A GOLDEN CONNECTION

You Cannot Succeed Alone.
Relationship is a *command.*
Relationship is a *privilege.*
Relationship is *unavoidable.*
Relationship can be the Golden Link to every uncommon miracle and experience of joy in your life. "Two are better than one; because they have a good reward for their labour. For if they fall, the one will lift up his fellow: but woe to him that is alone when he falleth; for he hath not another to help him up. Again, if two lie together, then they have heat: but how can one be warm alone? And if one prevail against him, two shall withstand him; and a threefold cord is not quickly broken," (Ecclesiastes 4:9-12).

The Most Powerful Law In The Universe Requires Two. Nothing is more effective on the earth against demonic spirits than the Law of Agreement. "Again I say unto you, That if two of you shall agree on earth as touching any thing that they shall ask, it shall be done for them of My Father which is in Heaven. For where two or three are gathered together in My name, there am I in the midst of them," (Matthew 18:19-20).

Five kinds of Relationships are necessary to

complete your Assignment on earth:

▶ Mentors – who *change* you.
▶ Protegés – who *challenge* you.
▶ Friends – who *comfort* you.
▶ Enemies – who *reward* you.
▶ Golden Connections – who *link* you.

Recognition of your Golden Connection can unleash waves of uncommon favor and miracles in your life. If you fail to recognize them as a gift from God, you will abort a thousand miracles.

30 Facts You Should Know About Your Golden Connection

1. A Golden Connection Is Any Person God Uses To Link You To A Desired Change.

2. You Cannot Succeed Without A Golden Connection. God uses them. God will never permit you to succeed alone (read Ecclesiastes 4:9-12).

3. Your Golden Connection May Not Necessarily Be A Personal Friend. The butler forgot Joseph for two years. The crisis of Pharaoh stimulated his memory. He did not consider himself a friend to Joseph, though Joseph was used of the Lord in his life. God used the butler to *link* Joseph to Pharaoh.

4. The Golden Connection May Be Your Link For A Moment, Not Your Lifetime. Philip was the Golden Link of the Ethiopian eunuch to God, yet we never see any relationship again beyond the day of their conversation (Acts 8).

5. The Golden Connection May Require Your Pursuit Of Them. Naomi was the Golden

Connection between Ruth and Boaz. Ruth pursued *her*. "Entreat me not to leave thee, or to return from following after thee: for whither thou goest, I will go; and where thou lodgest, I will lodge: thy people shall be my people, and thy God my God," (Ruth 1:16).

6. The Golden Connection May Attempt To Discourage Your Relationship With Them. Naomi instructed Ruth, "Return thou after thy sister in law," (Ruth 1:15). Ruth refused to accept any discouragement. She was persistent.

7. Those Around You May Attempt To Stop Your Relationship With The Golden Connection. When the blind man cried out to Jesus, he was instructed by those around him to keep silent. But, he *recognized* Jesus was his Golden Connection to his healing. His persistence created the relationship.

8. The Golden Connection May Be Intimidating To You. When Mordecai requested Esther to approach the king, she was mortified. It was forbidden to enter the presence of the king uninvited, but her desired future was stronger than her sense of inferiority. You must recognize that your *future* is more important than your *feelings*.

9. The Golden Connection May Not Even Recognize Themselves As Your Golden Connection. Boaz did not pursue Ruth. Ruth recognized him as The Golden Connection, and made herself accessible to him (Ruth 3:7-18).

10. The Golden Connection May Appear Disinterested In Your Relationship With Them. The woman who had an issue of blood for twelve years "pressed toward Jesus." He did not pursue her. She reached for Him. He seemed oblivious to her.

When she was healed, Jesus perceived that virtue left Him, "Who touched My clothes?" (Mark 5:30).

11. It Is Your Responsibility To Recognize The Golden Connection, Not Their Responsibility To Recognize You. The woman with the problem of the issue of blood recognized Jesus. He did not recognize her until *after* the healing (Mark 5:25-34).

12. The Golden Connection May Not Become Obvious Until Years Later. The butler was the link to Pharaoh, but he forgot Joseph for two years. The intercession of Abraham brought deliverance to Lot *after* they parted company (Genesis 19:29).

13. The Golden Connection May Be Discerned Instantly. It happened between David and Jonathan. As David finished speaking to King Saul, his son, Jonathan, was instantly knitted to the heart of David. "And it came to pass, when he had made an end of speaking unto Saul, that the soul of Jonathan was knit with the soul of David, and Jonathan loved him as his own soul," (1 Samuel 18:1).

14. The Golden Connection May Happen Quickly With Someone You Have Never Met Before. When Philip saw the Ethiopian eunuch in the chariot, he asked him if he understood the book he was reading. The eunuch immediately "desired Philip that he would come up and sit with him," (Acts 8:31). Though they had never met before, the connection occurred instantly.

15. Your Golden Connection May Not Recognize Your Value Until The Passage Of Time. Paul was The Golden Connection to John Mark for ministry. Paul became agitated with John

Mark and sought separation from him. "And Barnabas determined to take with them John, whose surname was Mark. But Paul thought not good to take him with them, who departed from them from Pamphylia, and went not with them to the work. And the contention was so sharp between them, that they departed asunder one from the other: and so Barnabas took Mark, and sailed unto Cyprus; And Paul chose Silas, and departed," (Acts 15:37-40).

As time passed, John Mark proved himself. Paul observed it. Later, the Apostle Paul writes a remarkable request to Timothy. "Only Luke is with me. Take Mark, and bring him with thee: for he is profitable to me for the ministry," (2 Timothy 4:11).

16. The Golden Connection May Be Nameless, Powerless And Even Appear Insignificant. A fascinating scenario in Scripture concerns a *nameless* handmaiden, brought in as a captive from Israel into the land of Syria. She was the handmaiden of the wife of a great general, Naaman. Yet, a single statement from her mouth unlocked one of the most remarkable miracles—the healing of leprosy. Naaman, captain of the army, had leprosy. The handmaiden told his wife, "Would God my lord were with the prophet that is in Samaria! for he would recover him of his leprosy," (2 Kings 5:3). The miracle made history (2 Kings 5:14). Sometimes, our greatest gifts from God arrive in the simplest packaging.

17. Your Access To The Golden Connection May Be Opposed. Queen Esther was The Golden Connection between the king and the deliverance of the Jews. Haman was their Enemy. There will always be someone who despises your relationship to your Golden Connection. Sometimes, your Enemy may be a silent one. You may not even know that someone is your Enemy. But, if you have a Golden Connection right now in your life, satan will stir someone up to break the relationship.

18. The Purpose Of The Golden Connection Is To Perpetuate And Complete The Plan Of God For Your Life. God has planned your future. He links you with those who will help you make changes. The butler perpetuated The Plan by linking Joseph to Pharaoh in the palace.

19. The Golden Connection May Affect The Survival Of An Entire Nation. Queen Esther, The Golden Connection between the king and the Jews, gave the Jews the right to defend themselves during the attempted annihilation. The entire nation survived, because of one lady.

20. The Golden Connection May Usher In A New Generation Of Champions. Read the life of Ruth. Naomi was her Golden Connection to Boaz. Their marriage birthed Obed, whose son was Jesse. Jesse produced David, who ushered in Solomon and the lineage of Jesus. It is true—a single Golden Connection can affect a thousand generations.

21. The Golden Connection May Be Burdensome, Difficult And Even Irritating. The butler *forgot* Joseph for two years. Naomi *discouraged* Ruth from pursuing her.

22. God Will Often Confirm Your Golden Connection. The servant of Abraham asked for this confirmation from God. His role was to secure a wife for Isaac, the son of Abraham. He prayed, "And let it come to pass, that the damsel to whom I shall say,

Let down thy pitcher, I pray thee, that I may drink; and she shall say, Drink, and I will give thy camels drink also: let the same be she that Thou hast appointed for Thy servant Isaac; and *thereby shall I know* that Thou hast shewed kindness unto my master," (Genesis 24:14).

23. The Golden Connection Is Often Someone Who Will Solve An Immediate Crisis In Your Life. When Haman processed a plan to annihilate the Jews, God used Esther as the Golden Connection to solve the crisis. Her boldness and presentation to the king gave the Jews the right to defend themselves.

24. The Golden Connection May Require You To Do Something You Have Never Done Before. Without Mordecai as her Golden Connection, Esther could have been destroyed herself through Haman's horrifying plan and hatred. Mordecai demanded she approach the king, even though she was uninvited. She did so and was saved (Esther 4:8).

25. The Golden Connection May Require You To Do Something Uncomfortable Or Difficult. Mordecai required Esther to approach the king uninvited. *It could have brought her death* (Esther 4:11). Elijah boldly instructed the widow to provide him *the very last meal* she had in her home (1 Kings 17). Ruth had to *leave the comfort* of Moab, to stay in the company of her Golden Connection, Naomi.

26. The Golden Connection May Be Used By God To Prevent A Tragedy In Your Life. Esther was The Link that *stopped the annihilation* of Jews. Elijah was The Link that prevented the death of the widow and her son during the famine. Jonah *stopped the destruction* of Nineveh through his message to them.

27. Your Golden Connection May Be Someone Completely The Opposite Of You. Goliath was the link between David and Saul. Naomi was the link between Ruth and Boaz. Philip was the link between the Ethiopian eunuch and God. God often sends someone to your life completely the opposite of you...to become The Golden Link to your next season.

28. God Often Uses The Golden Connection To Expose A Flaw Or Reveal A Mistake You Are Making. Nineveh was targeted for destruction, but God used Jonah to expose their sin. Tragedy was averted. "Arise, go unto Nineveh, that great city, and preach unto it the preaching that I bid thee," (Jonah 3:2). God sees more than your mistakes. He sees your greatness, your future. Nineveh sinned terribly against God. Yet, God called them "that great city."

29. Any Golden Connection That Is Disrespected Will Exit Your Life. Paul was a marvelous Golden Connection between the people and The Holy Spirit. When he spoke for three months concerning the Kingdom of God, some became hardened. They spoke evil against him and his teaching. God moved him away from them. "But when divers were hardened, and believed not, but spake evil of that way before the multitude, he *departed from them,* and separated the disciples, disputing daily in the school of one Tyrannus," (Acts 19:9).

30. When God Sends A Golden Connection Into Your Life He Is Creating Changes That Benefit You.

▶ Ministers are Golden Connections to *Changes.*

▶ Parents are Golden Connections to *Growth.*

▶ Bosses are Golden Connections to *Provision.*

Recognition Of The Golden Connection Is One Of The Greatest Secrets Of Increase Ever Discovered.

RECOMMENDED BOOKS AND TAPES ON THIS TOPIC

B-14   Seeds of Wisdom on Relationships (32 pages/$3)

B-44   31 Secrets for Career Success (114 pages/$10)

B-49   The Proverbs 31 Woman (70 pages/$7)

B-57   Thirty-One Secrets of an Unforgettable Woman (140 pages/$9)

B-82   31 Reasons People Do Not Receive Their Financial Harvest (252 pages/$12)

B-99   Secrets of the Richest Man Who Ever Lived (179 pages/$10)

TS-16   The Double Diamond Principle in Successful Relationships (6 tapes/$30)

TS-25   Secrets of the Richest Man Who Ever Lived (6 tapes/$30)

TS-37   31 Secrets of The Uncommon Mentor (6 tapes/$30)

TS-38   31 Reasons People Do Not Receive Their Financial Harvest (6 tapes/$30)

TS-53   Thirty-One Secrets of an Unforgettable Woman (6 tapes/$30)

"See then that ye walk circumspectly, not as fools, but as wise, Redeeming the time, because the days are evil."
Ephesians 5:15-16

❦ 25 ❦

RECOGNITION OF THE GIFT OF TIME

━━━➣•O•⬝━━━

Time Is Your Gift From God.

Time is creative. An acorn cooperates with Time and becomes an oak tree. Babies becomes leaders, affecting millions.

I have studied the biographies of champions for many years. The major difference that I observed between the prosperous and the poor is *the Valuing of Time.* When you drive to the ghetto, you will see healthy men and women casually sitting on the steps talking for hours. Garbage is strewn everywhere. Disorder is rampant. They have chosen to invest their time in trivia, while the prosperous are *working.*

An incredible illustration comes to my mind. Someone once wrote that a five-pound bar of iron, used three different ways, creates three different levels of income. If you turn the five-pound bar of iron into horseshoes, the value of the horseshoes would be $20-$40. If you used the same bar of iron to create needles instead, it might be worth $100 or more. But, if you decided to use the five-pound bar of iron to create watch springs, *the value of those watch springs would be over $3,000.*

Time has the same power. Some men use Time

to create $10. Others do something different with that hour and create $3,000.

In my book, *Secrets of the Richest Man Who Ever Lived,* chapter 17 is one of the most powerful chapters on Time you will ever read. I quote, "A major difference exists between the poor, the pauper and the prosperous. That difference is the Management of Time."

I cannot change your financial worth until I persuade you concerning *the Value of Time.*

I cannot improve your marriage relationship unless you realize *the Value of moments of Time.*

I cannot unlock the mystery of uncommon ministry until you are convinced of *the Value of a simple hour* of your Time.

The rich do not receive more than 24 hours a day. The poor do not receive less than 24 hours a day. Both are given *the same gift* from God—24 hours each day.

Every human has received the same amount of Time. The difference is how *you* choose to *invest* your Time.

6 Facts You Should Know About Managing Your Time

1. Anything Significant In Your Life Will Require The Investment Of Time. When you hurry, you will increase the mistakes in your life.

2. Time Invested In Preparation Will Repay You A Thousand Times Over. That is why years are invested in the designing of a single automobile...for long-range financial rewards.

Jesus referred to those who took the *Time* to

invest in the foundation of a house on a rock were wise.

3. Any Time You Invest In Restoration Of Your Energy And Physical Fitness Will Produce Unforgettable Benefits To You.

4. Your Attitude Toward Time Is Revealed Every Time You Make An Appointment With Someone. Precision communicates your respect for time. Punctuality sends a message—"Time matters to me."

5. It Is Your Responsibility To Train Those Around You To Respect Your Time. You do so by respecting their own Time as well. Recently, I had to cancel an appointment. When I finally appeared for the appointment the next week, I paid the man for the previous week's appointment, too. Integrity required it.

6. Successful Negotiations Will Always Require The Investment Of Time. Those who overcome the temptation to hurry...always control the transaction.

5 Tips In Making Your Time Count

1. Keep A Visual List Of Your Goals Before You At All Times. It may be in your notebook or on the walls of your office. What You See Determines What You Will Pursue.

2. Establish A Time Limit On Every Appointment. Set your appointment for 10:00-10:20, instead of simply saying, "I will see you around 10:00." *Precision Electrifies Any Environment.*

3. Always Stay In Movement Toward Your Next Appointment Or Goal. Those acquainted with the late President John F. Kennedy stated that every time someone was in his presence, they were conscious that he was moving *toward* an appointment with someone else. Though he did not appear hurried, he was *in movement.* This caused those around him to *treasure each moment* and make that moment count in their communication with him.

4. Mark Those Who Consistently Disrespect Your Time. If they do not respect your Time, your Wisdom will not be respected either.

5. Develop The Habit Of Looking At Your Watch Often. It educates others regarding the Value of your Time with them.

"To every thing there is a season, and a time to every purpose under the heaven," (Ecclesiastes 3:1).

"There is a time there for every purpose and for every work," (Ecclesiastes 3:17).

"See then that ye walk circumspectly, not as fools, but as wise, Redeeming the time, because the days are evil," (Ephesians 5:15-16).

Recognition Of The Miracle Gift Of Time Will Multiply Your Productivity, Increase Your Financial Worth And Make Every Moment Of Relationships More Valued.

RECOMMENDED BOOKS AND TAPES ON THIS TOPIC

B-44   31 Secrets for Career Success (114 pages/$10)
B-91   The Leadership Secrets of Jesus (196 pages/$10)
B-96   Secrets of The Journey, Vol. 5 (32 pages/$5)
B-99   Secrets of the Richest Man Who Ever Lived (179 pages/$10)
B-103   Secrets of The Journey, Vol. 7 (32 pages/$5)
TS-25   Secrets of the Richest Man Who Ever Lived (6 tapes/$30)

～ 26 ～

RECOGNITION OF YOUR PERSONAL LIMITATIONS

━━━━━◆━━━━━

You Cannot Do Everything.

You can only do what God *designed* you to do through your gifts, skills and intelligence.

Trees do not talk.

Turtles cannot fly.

Design determines your capability.

I love motivation seminars. Encouraging tapes have been a part of my life for many years. It is sad when someone misinterprets the teaching and attempts for many years to accomplish a dream God never birthed within them.

Persistence is the difference only *when the goal is one designed by God.*

Inexperienced airplane pilots have crashed, because they failed to recognize their personal limitations.

Inexperienced ministers have sometimes given unwise counsel, because they did not recognize their personal limitations.

Inexperienced police officers have sometimes refused to call for backup. Their deaths become evidence that they refused to recognize their personal limitations.

9 Facts About Your
Personal Limitations

In my book, *Secrets of the Richest Man Who Ever Lived,* I list facts you should know about your personal limitations. Let me share several that are important at this point.

1. Life Was Created To Be A Collection Of Relationships. Somebody sees what you cannot see. Somebody can do what you are incapable of doing. Arrogance deprives you of the incredible contribution others desire to give.

2. When You Fail To Recognize Your Personal Limitations, You Become Blind To The Gifts Hidden In Those Near You.

3. Recognition Of Your Personal Limitations Will Birth An Ability To Discern Opportunities Around You. You will always pursue something you lack.

4. Recognition Of Your Personal Limitations Will Unlock Compassion Toward You. Everyone relates to weakness. Admitting it unleashes Favor beyond your imagination. Vulnerability is a magnet for compassion.

5. Recognition Of Your Personal Limitations Will Expose Unnecessary Goals And Inappropriate Dreams You Have Collected Within You. You must learn to identify the important things from the lesser.

6. Recognition Of Your Personal Limitations Corrects Your Focus On What You Are Designed To Do. Broken Focus is the *real* reason men fail.

7. Recognition Of Your Personal Limitations Removes Stress. Nothing is more difficult than attempting to be something you can never be.

8. When You Fail To Recognize Your Personal Limitations, You Stop Seeking Solutions For Them. Your weakness will multiply. You Can Only Correct What You Are Willing To Confront.

9. Whatever You Do Not Possess Has Been Carefully Stored In Earthen Vessels Near You. Love Is The Master Key To Any House Of Treasure.

Recognition Of Your Personal Limitations Will Unlock The Unlimited Treasure Stored In Those Around You.

RECOMMENDED BOOKS AND TAPES ON THIS TOPIC
B-18   Seeds of Wisdom on Habits (32 pages/$3)
B-58   The Mentor's Manna on Attitude (32 pages/$3)
B-96   Secrets of The Journey, Vol. 5 (32 pages/$5)
B-99   Secrets of the Richest Man Who Ever Lived (179 pages/$10)
TS-14   How to Stay Motivated to Achieve Your Dream (6 tapes/$30)
TS-25   Secrets of the Richest Man Who Ever Lived (6 tapes/$30)
TS-52   The Assignment: The Dream & The Destiny (6 tapes/$30)

"For He remembered that they were
but flesh."
Pslam 78:39

❧ 27 ❧

RECOGNITION OF THE LIMITATIONS OF OTHERS

The Perfect Would Find You Unbearable.

Everyone has weaknesses and limitations. Your responsibility is to discern them.

Elsewhere I mentioned my tragic mistake of firing a young lady I dearly loved. Her gift was *enthusiasm,* not administration. She headed my music company and was in continuous contact with major recording artists. They adored her. They enjoyed her. She created many relationships for my ministry and life. When they talked to her, they had warm feelings toward me though I had never met many of them face-to-face.

Joy was her gift.

My failure to recognize her personal limitations created an undue burden on her. I kept giving her tasks to do, letters to type, files to create. Her loyalty to me created a *reluctance* in her to admit her limitations to me. She wanted to please me desperately. Subconsciously, she felt that any admission of limitation would lessen my admiration of her.

Sometimes, we interpret our discerning of the limitations of those around us as being critical. Our attempt to stay positive and upbeat often prevents an *accurate* assessment of others.

Here Are 5 Helpful Facts In Observing The Limitations Of Others

1. Every Human Contains Limitations. You are not God. Nobody else is either. Admit it.

2. Avoid A Critical Spirit When Discussing The Limitations Of Others With Them. Separate them from their mistakes. Reassure them of your love for them and your admiration of them. Every single personality is *used of the Lord* to accomplish His desired Assignment for them.

3. Focus On The Strengths Of Others, Not Their Personal Limitations. Somebody has something you lack. Do not lose it through a critical spirit. Locate that "good thing" within them.

4. Channel Any Task Or Work Expectations Toward Their Strength, Away From Their Personal Limitations. Recently, I asked a great pastor how he would handle someone who was consistently creating a different way of doing things than the instruction required. He said, "I have a lady who is very faithful. She is lovable and adorable, but she will always do something completely different than what I said. So, I move her as far away from me as possible in her work tasks. *Others* can work around her and with her...regardless of those personal limitations."

5. Do Not Discard The Faithful Because Of A Flaw. You will never achieve anything in your life if you are waiting to work with the unflawed.

Recognition Of The Limitations In Others Will Salvage Valuable Friendships, Prevent Heartache And Enable You To Unlock The Best In Others.

ᔷ 28 ᔷ

RECOGNITION OF
SPECIFIC ANOINTINGS

An Assignment Requires An Anointing.

The Anointing is the power of God provided us to remove a burden or destroy a yoke of bondage existing on another (Isaiah 61:1-4; 10:27 and Isaiah 14).

Specific Assignments require specific anointings.

A *leadership* anointing enables you to *love.*

An *administrative* anointing produces *order.*

A *healing* anointing releases *health.*

A *Psalmist* anointing unlocks *worship.*

A *Wisdom* anointing *illuminates.* "For the Word of God is quick, and powerful, and sharper than any two-edged sword, piercing even to the dividing asunder of soul and spirit, and of the joints and marrow, and is a discerner of the thoughts and intents of the heart," (Hebrews 4:12).

A *prophetic* anointing *reveals the will of God.*

2 Tragedies In The Body Of Christ

1. Many Never Walk In Joy And Do Not Sense The Pleasure Of Achievement Because They Have Not *Recognized* The Anointing God Has Placed On Their Own Life. They do not recognize *how God has chosen to use them in the lives of others.*

2. Many Never Receive Miracles Or Blessings Because They Do Not Respect And Celebrate The *Difference* Of The Anointings God Has Placed On Those Near Them. They do not discern how God desires to use *others* to bless *them.*

13 Important Keys In Understanding The Anointing That Flows Through Your Life And Others

1. The Anointing Is The Power Of God. "And it shall come to pass in that day, that His burden shall be taken away from off thy shoulder, and His yoke from off thy neck, and the yoke shall be destroyed because of the anointing," (Isaiah 10:27).

2. The Anointing Is The Power Of God To Conquer Any Enemy That Emerges In Your Life. "How God anointed Jesus of Nazareth with the Holy Ghost and with power: Who went about doing good, and healing all that were oppressed of the devil; for God was with Him," (Acts 10:38).

3. You Always Possess Something God Desires To Anoint. Moses had a rod. David had a slingshot. Surrender increases your dependence on God.

4. Your Success In Life Or Ministry Will Depend On The Anointing You Choose To Respect. Zacchaeus recognized the difference in Jesus. Jesus bonded with him because of it.

5. The Anointing Increases In Your Life Proportionate To Your Dependence On God.

Your prayer life reveals your humility or pride. Any attempt to accomplish anything apart from God eventually paralyzes the flow of that anointing through you. "But the manifestation of the Spirit is given to every man to profit withal," (1 Corinthians 12:7).

6. An Increase Of The Anointing Will Increase Order In Your Life. "Let all things be done decently and in order," (1 Corinthians 14:40). "For God is not the author of confusion, but of peace, as in all churches of the saints," (1 Corinthians 14:33).

7. The Anointing Turns Common Things Into Uncommon Weapons. The simple rod of Moses became a snake. Stretched over the Red Sea, it divided the waters. The simple slingshot of David destroyed Goliath, and ushered David into kingship.

8. The Anointing That Attracts Some Often Alienates Others. "Think not that I am come to send peace on earth: I came not to send peace, but a sword. For I am come to set a man at variance against his father, and the daughter against her mother, and the daughter in law against her mother in law. And a man's foes shall be they of his own household," (Matthew 10:34-36).

When you obey The Holy Spirit, some will withdraw from you.

9. The Anointing Is Determined By The Will Of God, Not Your Perfection. "For I know that in me (that is, in my flesh,) dwelleth no good thing," (Romans 7:18).

10. Any Destructive Act Against The Anointed Is Forbidden In Scripture. "Touch not Mine anointed, and do My prophets no harm," (Psalm 105:15). It is dangerous to speak slanderously of men God is using greatly.

11. Your Respect For The Anointing Will Create Access To It. During the famine, Elijah was sent only to the widow, *who respected his counsel.* Jesus went home with Zacchaeus, because of *the respect* he had toward Jesus. "And when Jesus came to the place, He looked up, and saw him, and said unto him, Zacchaeus, make haste, and come down; for today I must abide at thy house," (Luke 19:5).

12. Your Respect For The Anointing On Others Increases The Blessing Of God Upon Your Life. The widow respected Elijah and experienced abundant provision through a famine (1 Kings 17). David respected the anointing on Saul and received the kingship. Joshua respected the anointing on Moses and received his inheritance.

13. The Anointing You Respect Is The Anointing That Will Grow In Your Life. The respect of Joshua for Moses moved Joshua into leadership.

When you respect the anointing for *healing,* miracles of healing will flow. When you respect an anointing for *financial breakthrough,* debt can be eliminated. When you respect an anointing for *Wisdom,* ideas and favor will flow like unstoppable currents.

In my book, *The Holy Spirit Handbook,* chapter 11 contains 18 facts you should know about The Anointing. I urge you to read this powerful and revealing book.

A Special Note

One of the tragedies in our present generation is the disrespect toward the financial anointing resting on a few leaders. Few Financial Deliverers exist in the body of Christ. Those who walk in the *center* of that focus and abandon themselves completely to that calling often become the focus of ridicule, contempt and even anger.

"But, Mike, that preacher on television only talks about finances the entire program! He never talks about anything else! He should be balanced!" Someone complained to me.

"Are you angry at the dentist because he refuses to mow your grass?" I asked. "Are you mad at your lawyer because he will not pull your teeth when they hurt? Are you angry at the evangelist who preaches salvation but does not have a healing line for the sick? Are you angry about the veterinarian who will not become a contractor and build an extra room on your house? Is your eye angry because the ear refuses to see?"

Function is determined by God. Not us.

One lady was very upset with her pastor because he spoke on financial keys for 15 minutes before the offering was received in her church. "I cannot believe my own pastor talked about money for 15 minutes on Sunday morning!" she said.

I asked her how many hours it took for her to get dressed each morning, the drive to her job, the hours she worked each day and the time it took to drive back home in the evening traffic. The total hours she spent involved in her work was 55 hours each week.

"Explain something to me," I requested. "Why are you angry with a pastor who encourages you for 15-minutes a week to *expect* financial blessing when you have invested 55 hours of your life that week in pursuit of money?"

The criticism toward Financial Deliverers is *demonic.*

Patients rarely hate their Healers.

If you are critical toward healing ministries, do not expect the wave of healing to flow into your house.

If you are critical toward financial ministries, do not expect ideas for financial blessing to explode within you.

If you defy the anointing of those in authority over you, do not expect the rewards of protection, provision and promotion.

What You Respect Will Move Toward You.

What You Disrespect Will Move Away From You.

Recognition Of The Unique Anointing Of God On Others Could Increase Your Own Anointing One Thousand Times More (Deuteronomy 1:11).

RECOMMENDED BOOKS AND TAPES ON THIS TOPIC

B-74   The Assignment: The Dream & The Destiny, Vol. 1 (164 pages/$10)

B-75   The Assignment: The Anointing & The Adversity, Vol. 2 (192 pages/$10)

B-91   The Leadership Secrets of Jesus (196 pages/$10)

B-97   The Assignment: The Trials & The Triumphs, Vol. 3 (160 pages/$10)

B-98   The Assignment: The Pain & The Passion, Vol. 4 (144 pages/$10)

B-100 The Holy Spirit Handbook, Vol. 1 (153 pages/$10)

TS-29 The Holy Spirit Handbook (6 tapes/$30)

TS-37 31 Secrets of the Uncommon Mentor (6 tapes/$30)

TS-52 The Assignment: The Dream & The Destiny (6 tapes/$30)

∝ 29 ∝

RECOGNITION OF THE PROBLEM YOU ARE PRESENTLY ASSIGNED TO SOLVE

━━━━━━━━➣•◦•◄━━━━━━━

You Were Created To Solve A Problem.

Doctors solve physical problems. Mothers solve emotional problems. Dentists solve teeth problems. Mechanics solve car problems. Everything God created was created to solve an existing problem.

Millions of problems exist on the earth. Solving those problems provides income, favor and the flow of financial provision for the billions living on the earth.

Thousands remain impoverished because they have not recognized the problem closest to them that needs to be solved. Millions will never receive promotion because they ignore the problem closest to them. *Marriages* have deteriorated because a mate *refused to recognize* the problem closest to them.

> ▶ The Problem Closest To You Is The Golden Gate Out Of Trouble.
> ▶ The Problem Closest To You Is Your Secret Code To The Throne.

When Joseph solved the problem nearest him, he

moved into his next season of promotion.

46 Important Facts You Should Know About Problem Solving

1.   You Were Created To Solve A Problem. "To rejoice in his labour; this is the gift of God," (Ecclesiastes 5:19).

2.   The Problem You Solve Provides The Provision For Your Life. "And also that every man should eat and drink, and enjoy the good of all his labour, it is the gift of God," (Ecclesiastes 3:13).

3.   The Problem That Infuriates You The Most Is Often The Problem God Has Assigned You To Solve. When Moses observed an Egyptian beating an Israelite, anger arose. Anger is a clue, a signal that God wants you to *correct* something that grieves Him. Anger is the birthplace for change.

4.   Your Gifts And Skills Are Clues To The Problem You Were Created To Solve. You may be gifted with numbers, working with children or administration. Your gift is revealed by what you *love*. The Proof Of Love Is The Investment Of *Time*. What you are willing to invest time in learning is a clue to an existing gift within you.

5.   Uncommon   Men   Often   Solve Uncommon Problems. Those who design skyscrapers have a different creativity than those who build doghouses. The pay differs, too!

6.   Uncommon Men Often Solve Common Problems In An Uncommon Way. It is the secret of McDonald's, the largest hamburger restaurant chain on earth. Killing a man in battle is common, but David became known because he did it with an

Uncommon Weapon against an Uncommon Enemy.

7. You Will Only Be Remembered For The Problems You Solve Or The Ones You Create. Joseph is remembered because he solved the problem of provision during famine.

8. Uncommon Men Often Distinguish Themselves By The Method They Use To Solve A Problem. The leprosy of Naaman disappeared because of an illogical instruction from Elisha—"dip in Jordan seven times."

9. Currents Of Favor Will Flow Into Your Life The Moment You Solve A Problem For Somebody. When the Apostle Paul brought the healing power of God to the father of Publius, the chief of the island, Favor flowed. Others were healed. Then, the Apostle Luke documents, "Who also honoured us with many honours; and when we departed, they laded us with such things as were necessary," (Acts 28:10).

David pursued a knowledge of the reward for killing Goliath. "The king will enrich him with great riches, and will give him his daughter, and make his father's house free in Israel," (1 Samuel 17:25).

10. The Problem You Solve Determines The Salary You Earn. Lawyers make $200 an hour while a gardener earns $8 an hour. Both men are worthy. The problem they have chosen to solve has a different value.

11. Never Discuss A Problem With Those Incapable Of Solving It. Their answers will incense you.

12. The Problem You Solve For Others Determines The Problems God Will Solve For

You. "Knowing that whatsoever good thing any man doeth, the same shall he receive of the Lord, whether he be bond or free," (Ephesians 6:8).

13. The Blessing Of The Lord Will Always Be Proportionate To The Problem You Have Chosen To Solve. "The Lord shall open unto thee His good treasure, the Heaven to give the rain unto thy land in His season, and to bless all the work of thine hand," (Deuteronomy 28:12).

14. Those Who Refuse To Solve Problems Should Not Be Supported By Those Who Do. "For even when we were with you, this we commanded you, that if any would not work, neither should he eat," (2 Thessalonians 3:10).

15. Scriptures Forbid Intimacy And Relationship With Those Who Are Unwilling To Work And Solve Problems. "For we hear that there are some which walk among you disorderly, working not at all, but are busybodies...note that man, and have no company with him, that he may be ashamed," (2 Thessalonians 3:11-14).

16. Those Skilled In Solving Problems Are Qualified To Rule Over Others. "The hand of the diligent shall bear rule: but the slothful shall be under tribute," (Proverbs 12:24).

17. Uncommon Problem Solvers Are Pursued By Uncommon Men Of Greatness. "Seest thou a man diligent in his business? he shall stand before kings," (Proverbs 22:29).

18. Solving A Problem Cheerfully Increases Favor. "A merry heart doeth good like a medicine," (Proverbs 17:22).

19. Your Flexibility And Willingness To

Solve A Problem Affects Your Salary And Respect Received. Twenty-four hour cafes exist because of *flexibility*.

20. Many Eventually Hear About The Problem You Solve For Others. Boaz knew that Ruth treated Naomi better than seven sons would treat their mother.

21. God Expects You To Observe And Recognize The Problem Nearest You. "But whoso hath this world's good, and seeth his brother have need, and shutteth up his bowels of compassion from him, how dwelleth the love of God in him?" (1 John 3:17).

22. God Expects You To Solve The Problem Nearest You. "Withhold not good from them to whom it is due, when it is in the power of thine hand to do it," (Proverbs 3:27). Joseph applied this to the butler.

23. Your Assignment Determines The Kinds Of Problems You Notice And Desire To Solve. Tailors notice missing buttons. Hairstylists notice your hair. Mechanics *hear* something wrong in your car engine. Why? That is their Assignment. Your Assignment heightens and *magnifies* the problems you notice and are called to solve.

24. You Are Not Assigned To Solve Problems For Everybody. Determine to whom you have been assigned. Jesus told the Pharisees that He was not called to those who were whole, but to those who realized they were sick and needed Him.

25. You Are Not Assigned To Solve Every Kind Of Problem For Everyone. Pastors are not necessarily anointed to solve real estate problems, automobile breakdowns and estate planning. Others can do that.

26. Problems Are Catalysts That Cause Us To Reach For Each Other. You only call a dentist when your teeth hurt. You only call your lawyer about legal matters. Problems create relationships.

27. Problems Reveal The Value Of Those Nearest Us. Someone told me that when they went to the hospital, the love and caring of their loved ones meant more to them than ever.

28. The Problems Others Are Experiencing Often Cause Them To Recognize Your Value. Children that ignore parents will often reach during a crisis they encounter.

29. Your Phone Will Never Ring Unless Someone Has A Problem They Want You To Solve. It may be emotional reassurance, a piece of information or a question that requires answering. Problems initiate reaching.

30. Any Problem Created By Rebellion Can Only Be Solved By The Repentance Of The Rebellious. When non-tithers ask a minister to pray for their prosperity, it is futile and absurd for the minister to do so. Their repentance is the key to their prosperity. Likewise, it is foolish to support a son-in-law who is defying the Scriptural command to work.

31. The Holy Spirit Will Often Forbid You To Solve Problems For Specific People. Paul experienced this. "Now when they had gone throughout Phrygia and the region of Galatia, and were forbidden of the Holy Ghost to preach the word in Asia, After they were come to Mysia, they assayed to go into Bithynia: but the Spirit suffered them not," (Acts 16:6-7).

32. Those You Love Often Want You To Solve Their Problems Without Them Tasting The Painful Consequences Of Their Own Rebellion. I begged one pastor not to take on an unnecessary indebtedness. He was determined to build a palace before the people were present to pay for it. I pleaded with him. I insisted that he was "missing the will of God." He insisted. Then, when he proceeded, he begged me to come back and bail him out of the problem. The Holy Spirit forbade me.

33. Small Problems Are Often Signals That A Deeper Problem Exists. When a young couple stays in debt, it indicates that greed runs deep. Their unwillingness to wait reveals impatience. Impatience has caused more debt than we could ever imagine.

34. You Cannot Solve Problems For Anyone In Rebellion Against God. "But if ye refuse and rebel, ye shall be devoured with the sword: for the mouth of the Lord hath spoken it," (Isaiah 1:20).

Never breathe life into something God is killing.

Never kill something God is resurrecting.

Permit God to complete His plan in others around you.

35. You Cannot Solve A Problem For Someone Who Distrusts Your Ability To Do So. "He that cometh to God must believe that He is, and that He is a rewarder of them that diligently seek Him," (Hebrews 11:6).

36. You Can Only Solve A Problem For The

Person Who Knows He Has One. God cannot even save someone who does not realize they are lost. Confession is a necessity. The Pharisees refused to acknowledge they had a problem. It cost them eternity.

37. The Problems Of Others Are Not The Commands Of God To Get Involved. You must develop the ability to hear The Voice of The Spirit, instead of responding to the expectations of people.

Rebellion creates *crisis.*

Continuous rebellion creates *continuous* crisis.

Unending rebellion creates *unending* crisis.

Many parents want to cushion the fall when their rebellious teenagers defy the Scriptures.

38. You Can Only Solve Problems For The Humble. The arrogant will alter your instructions. The rebellious will defy them. The prideful will ignore their problem. Confession indicates humility.

39. You Cannot Solve A Problem For The Unrepentant. Pharisees were unrepentant. Rebels are disqualified from receiving help.

40. You Cannot Help Anyone Who Does Not Trust Your Counsel. A relative asked me for counsel. I gave it. Then, they informed me that they had made a different decision. They asked me for *more* advice. I declined.

41. Those Who Disagree With Your Solution For Their Problem Disqualify Themselves For Additional Counsel. "To him that knoweth to do good, and doeth it not, to him it is sin," (James 4:17).

42. You Can Predict The Success Of Others By The Problem They Have Chosen To Solve.

Joseph chose to solve a problem for those nearest him. It guaranteed his access to Pharoah.

43. Somebody You Do Not Know Is Discussing The Problem You Are Capable Of Solving For Them. Never panic when you do not see the results of your efforts. Somewhere, you are being discussed. Boaz listened to his servants regarding Ruth and Naomi. He knew that she was better to a mother-in-law than seven sons would be to their mother.

44. Someone In Leadership Is Carefully Observing The Attitude With Which You Are Solving Your Present Problems. Boaz respected Ruth because of her attitude toward Naomi.

45. Money Is Merely A Reward For Solving A Problem. When you observe someone who never has any money—they obviously are not solving problems or solving them for the wrong person.

46. Everyone Has Problems They Are Incapable Of Solving. That is why the banker is necessary, the taxi driver, the brick layer, the truck driver and the psychologist. You are necessary...to someone.

Recognition Of The Problem Closest To You Is The Golden Exit From Your Chaos, The Golden Gate To The Throne And Will Catapult Your Life To Promotion.

RECOMMENDED BOOKS AND TAPES ON THIS TOPIC
B-39   The Double Diamond Principle (148 pages/$9)
B-40   Wisdom for Crisis Times (112 pages/$9)
B-44   31 Secrets for Career Success (114 pages/$10)
B-74   The Assignment: The Dream & The Destiny, Vol. 1 (164 pages/$10)
B-75   The Assignment: The Anointing & The Adversity, Vol. 2 (192 pages/$10)
B-82   31 Reasons People Do Not Receive Their Financial Harvest (252 pages/$12)

B-97   The Assignment: The Trials & The Triumphs, Vol. 3 (160 pages/ $10)
B-98   The Assignment: The Pain & The Passion, Vol. 4 (144 pages/$10)
B-101   The 3 Most Important Things in Your Life (240 pages/$10)
B-105   31 Days to Succeeding on Your Job (144 pages/$10)
TS-03   How to Walk Through Fire (6 tapes/$30)
TS-06   Secrets of the Greatest Achievers Who Ever Lived, Series 1 (6 tapes/ $30)
TS-07   Secrets of the Greatest Achievers Who Ever Lived, Series 2 (6 tapes/ $30)
TS-37   31 Secrets of the Uncommon Mentor (6 tapes/$30)
TS-38   31 Reasons People Do Not Receive Their Financial Harvest (6 tapes/$30)
TS-39   The Double Diamond Principle (6 tapes/$30)
TS-40   Wisdom for Crisis Times (6 tapes/$30)

≈ 30 ≈

RECOGNITION OF THOSE ASSIGNED TO YOU

———◆◆◆———

Somebody Is Assigned To Your Life.

Somewhere...*somebody*...feels *protective* toward you. They are willing to take on your battles. They want to be a Wall of Protection, a Source of nourishment and motivation for your life.

You cannot succeed alone. God never intended for you to live your life without relationships. Peter recognized this. "Then Simon Peter answered Him, Lord, to whom shall we go? Thou hast the words of eternal life," (John 6:68).

Mentors are assigned to impart to you. Elijah was assigned to Elisha. Paul felt the pain of Timothy. Moses advised Joshua. Mordecai felt accountable to reveal the plot to Esther.

Protegés are assigned to learn from you. They will not find anywhere else what God has placed within you for them. They *know* it.

21 Facts To Help You Identify Those Assigned To You

1. Each Person Assigned To You Will Solve A Different Problem For You. Some *motivate* you. Some *educate* you. Some *correct* you.

2. Those Assigned To You Will Proudly Identify With You Publicly. The critics of Elijah sneered at Elisha, his Protegé. Elisha instructed them to "hold ye your peace," (2 Kings 2:3).

3. Those Assigned To You Gladly Adjust Their Plans To Accommodate You During A Time Of Need.

4. Those Assigned To You Feel Protective Toward You. That is why Peter cut the ear off the soldier who raised his hand against his Lord.

5. Those Assigned To You Will Even Defend You In Your Absence. One young man told me that he had listened to an angry employee of mine criticize me for two hours. I explained to him the following:

The employee who criticized me felt *comfortable* in doing so in his presence *for a reason.* The critical employee was permitted to destroy my character for two hours indicating that The Listener was *unprotective* toward me. *Enemies are uncomfortable in attacking someone you truly love...while in your presence.*

6. Those Assigned To You Will Warn You Of Impending Danger And Traps Set By Enemies Or Adversarial People. Paul felt this kind of loyalty. "Therefore watch, and remember, that by the space of three years I ceased not to warn every one night and day with tears," (Acts 20:31).

7. Those Assigned To You Willingly Become Enemies To Your Enemies. Esther was assigned to save the nation of Jews. Haman was their Enemy. She became an Enemy to Haman because he was the Enemy to her people.

8. Those Who Are Assigned To You Will Never Enter Into A Covenant Of Friendship

With Anyone Plotting Your Destruction. "A friend loveth at all times, and a brother is born for adversity," (Proverbs 17:17).

9. Those Who Are Assigned To You Will Protect Your Reputation At Any Cost. Everybody makes mistakes. Those assigned to you *build a wall of protection.* Ruth honored the request of Boaz, "Let it not be known that a woman came into the floor," (Ruth 3:14).

10. Those Assigned To You Will Never Use Information To Hurt You. Jonathan would not reveal the hiding place of David to Saul, his father. It is the glory of a king "to conceal a matter." Love covers.

11. Those Assigned To You Willingly Forfeit The Rewards Of Other Relationships To Stay By Your Side. Jonathan walked away from the throne to stand by the side of David (1 Samuel 23:16-18).

12. Those Assigned To You Will Pay Any Price To Pleasure You (1 Chronicles 11:17-19).

13. Those Who Are Assigned To You Discern Your Greatness Even When Your Behavior Appears Unwise! David wanted to kill Nabal. Abigail reminded him of his future and his qualities of kingship. Those assigned to you will discern your greatness when your conduct seems the reverse.

14. Anyone Who Breaks Your Confidentiality Is Not Assigned To You.

15. Those Assigned To You Have Flaws. Their imperfection enables them to endure your imperfections, too!

16. Those Assigned To You May Sometimes Experience Doubts About Your Life And

Future. Thomas even doubted the presence of Jesus.

17. Those Assigned To You May Initially Dread Their Assignment To You. Jonah did not want to go to Nineveh, but "Seaweed University" *educated* him!

18. Those Assigned To You May Sometimes Disappoint You. Peter denied the Lord three times. Jesus saw beyond the denial.

19. Those Assigned To You May Sometimes Make You Impatient. "The Lord is good unto them that wait for Him," (Lamentations 3:25).

20. Those Assigned To You May Be Only For A Short Season. Jesus said, "I must needs to go through Samaria." It was a one-day experience for the Samaritan Woman but, it changed her forever.

21. Those Assigned To You Can Often Endure Stress You Cannot.

Stop long enough to appreciate those who have pressed toward your life.

Recognition Of Those Assigned To You Can Remove The Unnecessary Burdens And Responsibilities That Make Life Seem Unbearable.

RECOMMENDED BOOKS AND TAPES ON THIS TOPIC

B-14   Seeds of Wisdom on Relationships (32 pages/$3)
B-44   31 Secrets for Career Success (114 pages/$10)
B-49   The Proverbs 31 Woman (70 pages/$7)
B-57   Thirty-One Secrets of an Unforgettable Woman (140 pages/$9)
B-74   The Assignment: The Dream & The Destiny, Vol. 1 (164 pages/$10)
B-75   The Assignment: The Anointing & The Adversity, Vol. 2 (192 pages/$10)
B-86   The Gift of Wisdom for Leaders (32 pages/$10)
B-90   The Gift of Wisdom for Ministers (32 pages/$10)
B-95   Secrets of The Journey, Vol. 4 (32 pages/$5)
B-97   The Assignment: The Trials & The Triumphs, Vol. 3 (160 pages/$10)
B-98   The Assignment: The Pain & The Passion, Vol. 4 (144 pages/$10)
TS-24   31 Secrets of The Uncommon Problem-Solver (6 tapes/$30)
TS-52   The Assignment: The Dream & The Destiny (6 tapes/$30)
TS-53   Thirty-One Secrets of an Unforgettable Woman (6 tapes/$30)

≈ 31 ≈

RECOGNITION OF THE BIBLE AS YOUR MASTER SUCCESS HANDBOOK

The Bible Is The Master Success Handbook.

Your most difficult life habit to birth will be reading The Word of God every morning of your life. Yet, it is the Miracle Tool that produces changes your heart longs for.

12 Rewards Of Reading The Word Of God

1. The Word Of God Unleashes Your Very Life Within You. "It is the spirit that quickeneth; the flesh profiteth nothing: the words that I speak unto you, they are spirit, and they are life," (John 6:63). Life is energy. The Word Of God Creates Unexplainable Energy. "...quicken me according to Thy judgments," (Psalm 119:156).

2. The Word Of God Solves Your Mental Problems. "Great peace have they which love Thy law," (Psalm 119:165).

3. The Word Of God Cleanses Your Conscience. "Now ye are clean through the Word which I have spoken unto you," (John 15:3).

4. The Word Of God Purifies. "Wherewithal shall a young man cleanse his way? by taking heed thereto according to Thy word," (Psalm 119:9).

5. The Word Of God Corrects You. "All scripture is given by inspiration of God, and is profitable for doctrine, for reproof, for correction, for instruction in righteousness," (2 Timothy 3:16).

6. The Word Of God Solves Every Battle. "Thou through Thy commandments hast made me wiser than mine enemies," (Psalm 119:98).

7. The Word Of God Warns Of Pitfalls. "Thy word have I hid in mine heart, that I might not sin against Thee," (Psalm 119:11). "The wicked have laid a snare for me: yet I erred not from Thy precepts," (Psalm 119:110).

8. The Word Of God Drives Back The Darkness Around You. "The entrance of Thy Words giveth light," (Psalm 119:130).

9. The Word Of God Births Uncommon Joy. "These things have I spoken unto you, that My joy might remain in you, and that your joy might be full," (John 15:11).

10. The Word Of God Births The Fear Of God. Examples of judgment energize us to correct our conduct and change our behavior.

11. The Word Of God Creates A Hatred Of Evil. "Be not wise in thine own eyes: fear the Lord, and depart from evil," (Proverbs 3:7).

12. The Word Of God Is The Source Of Wisdom In Your Life. "For the Lord giveth wisdom; out of His mouth cometh knowledge and understanding," (Proverbs 2:6).

12 Rewards Of Wisdom

1. Wisdom Is The Master Key To All The Treasures Of Life. "And God said to Solomon, Because this was in thine heart, and thou hast not asked riches, wealth, or honour, nor the life of thine enemies, neither yet hast asked long life;...Wisdom and knowledge is granted unto thee; and I will give thee riches, and wealth, and honour, such as none of the kings have had that have been before," (2 Chronicles 1:11-12).

"In Whom are hid all the treasures of wisdom and knowledge" (Colossians 2:3).

2. The Fear Of God Is The Beginning Of Wisdom. "The fear of the Lord is the beginning of wisdom: and the knowledge of the holy is understanding," (Proverbs 9:10).

"The fear of the Lord is the beginning of wisdom," (Psalm 111:10).

"And unto man He said, Behold, the fear of the Lord, that is wisdom; and to depart from evil is understanding," (Job 28:28).

3. Wisdom Is More Powerful Than Weapons Of War. "Wisdom is better than weapons of war," (Ecclesiastes 9:18). "And wisdom and knowledge shall be the stability of thy times, and strength of salvation: the fear of the Lord is His treasure," (Isaiah 33:6).

"But the mouth of the upright shall deliver them," (Proverbs 12:6).

4. Right Relationships Increase Your Wisdom. "He that walketh with wise men shall be wise: but a companion of fools shall be destroyed," (Proverbs 13:20).

"Be not deceived: evil communications corrupt good manners," (1 Corinthians 15:33).

"Perverse disputings of men of corrupt minds, and destitute of the truth, supposing that gain is godliness: from such withdraw thyself," (1 Timothy 6:5).

5. Wisdom Is Better Than Jewels Or Money. "For wisdom is better than rubies; and all the things that may be desired are not to be compared to it," (Proverbs 8:11).

"Happy is the man that findeth wisdom, and the man that getteth understanding. For the merchandise of it is better than the merchandise of silver, and the gain thereof than fine gold. She is more precious than rubies; and all the things thou canst desire are not to be compared unto her," (Proverbs 3:13-15).

"For the price of wisdom is above rubies," (Job 28:18).

"How much better is it to get wisdom than gold! and to get understanding rather to be chosen than silver!" (Proverbs 16:16).

6. The Wise Welcome Correction. "Reprove not a scorner, lest he hate thee; rebuke a wise man, and he will love thee. Give instruction to a wise man, and he will be yet wiser: teach a just man, and he will increase in learning," (Proverbs 9:8-9).

"The ear that heareth the reproof of life abideth among the wise. He that refuseth instruction despiseth his own soul: but he that heareth reproof getteth understanding," (Proverbs 15:31-32).

"My son, despise not the chastening of the Lord; neither be weary of His correction. For whom the

Lord loveth He correcteth; even as a father the son in whom he delighteth," (Proverbs 3:11-12).

7. Wisdom Creates Currents Of Favor And Recognition Toward You. "Exalt her, and she shall promote thee: she shall bring thee to honour, when thou dost embrace her," (Proverbs 4:8).

"Blessed is the man that heareth Me, watching daily at My gates, waiting at the posts of My doors. For whoso findeth Me findeth life, and shall obtain favour of the Lord," (Proverbs 8:34-35).

"My son, forget not My law; So shalt thou find favour and good understanding in the sight of God and man," (Proverbs 3:1, 4).

8. Wisdom Guarantees Promotion. "By Me kings reign, and princes decree justice. By Me princes rule, and nobles, even all the judges of the earth," (Proverbs 8:15-16).

"And thou, Ezra, after the wisdom of thy God, that is in thine hand, set magistrates and judges, which may judge all the people that are beyond the river, all such as know the laws of thy God; and teach ye them that know them not," (Ezra 7:25).

"Exalt her, and she shall promote thee: she shall bring thee to honour, when thou dost embrace her. She shall give to thine head an ornament of grace: a crown of glory shall she deliver to thee," (Proverbs 4:8-9).

9. When You Increase Your Wisdom You Will Increase Your Wealth. "Riches and honour are with Me; yea durable riches and righteousness. That I may cause those that love Me to inherit substance; and I will fill their treasures," (Proverbs 8:18, 21).

"Length of days is in her right hand; and in her left hand riches and honour," (Proverbs 3:16).

"Blessed is the man that feareth the Lord, that delighteth greatly in His commandments. Wealth and riches shall be in his house," (Psalm 112:1, 3).

"The crown of the wise is their riches," (Proverbs 14:24).

10. Wisdom Makes Your Enemies Helpless Against You. "For I will give you a mouth and wisdom, which all your adversaries shall not be able to gainsay nor resist," (Luke 21:15).

"When a man's ways please the Lord, He maketh even his enemies to be at peace with him," (Proverbs 16:7).

"For wisdom is a defence, and money is a defence," (Ecclesiastes 7:12).

"For the Lord giveth wisdom: To deliver thee from the way of the evil man,...To deliver thee from the strange woman," (Proverbs 2:6, 12, 16).

11. Wisdom Can Be Imparted By The Laying On Of Hands Of A Man Of God. "Wherefore I put thee in remembrance that thou stir up the gift of God, which is in thee by the putting on of my hands. That good thing which was committed unto thee keep by the Holy Ghost which dwelleth in us," (2 Timothy 1:6, 14).

"And Joshua the son of Nun was full of the Spirit of wisdom; *for Moses had laid his hands upon him,*" (Deuteronomy 34:9).

"Whom they set before the apostles: and when they had prayed, they laid their hands on them. And Stephen, full of faith and power, did great wonders and miracles among the people. And they were not able to resist *the wisdom* and the Spirit by which he spake," (Acts 6:6, 8, 10).

12. The Word Of God Is Your Source Of Wisdom. "Behold I have taught you statutes and judgments, even as the Lord my God commanded me, that ye should do so in the land whither ye go to possess it. *For this is your wisdom* and your understanding in the sight of the nations," (Deuteronomy 4:5-6).

"Thou *through Thy commandments* hast made me wiser than mine enemies: for they are ever with me. I have more understanding than all my teachers: for Thy testimonies are my meditation. I understand more than the ancients, because I keep Thy precepts," (Psalm 119:98-100).

"For the Lord giveth *wisdom:* out of His mouth cometh knowledge and understanding," (Proverbs 2:6).

9 Helpful Hints In Reading The Word Of God

1. Read It Daily. What You Do *Daily* Determines What You Become Permanently.

2. Read It Prayerfully. The Holy Spirit will talk to you through His Word as you read it with a humble heart.

3. Read It Thoughtfully. Do not rush through it. Read each word as if it is pregnant with a secret coded message just for you. It is!

4. Read It Joyfully. Something is changing within you as His words enter you. The words of God are like time-release capsules entering the soil of your life, releasing incredible benefits and pleasure.

5. Read It Aloud. When I read The Word of God aloud, it affects me more than at any other time.

Sometimes, as a cassette tape of Scripture reading is playing, I will follow the reading along visually in my Bible. The effect is astounding. It multiplies the impact of The Word in your life.

6. Mark The Bible As You Read It. Color-code the Scriptures that mean the most to you. I use red to highlight Scriptures relating to the heartbeat of my life—The Holy Spirit, Jesus and The Word of God. Highlighted in *green* are the Scriptures relating to financial blessing. *Yellow* indicates Scriptures I have already memorized or desire to memorize. *Blue* indicates something of uncommon importance.

7. Wrap Every Telephone Conversation With A Scripture And Prayer. Your emphasis on The Word of God may be the *only* time your friend hears it.

8. Give The Word Of God As Special Gifts To Those You Love. That is why I created the Topical Bibles for Businessmen, Fathers, Mothers and Teenagers. I created an entire series called the *"One-Minute Pocket Bible"* for Mothers, Fathers and Businessmen. Nothing is more important than The Word.

9. Every Battle Against Your Life From Satan Is Designed To Separate You From The Word Of God. When satan alienates you from The Word, he has destroyed your only effective Defense.

> ▶ *Your Most Important Friend* Is The One Who Helps You Believe And Live The Word Of God.
> ▶ *Your Worst Enemy* Is Anyone Who Weakens Your Desire To Know And Obey The

Word Of God.

Recognition Of The Word Of God As Your Master Success Handbook Will Alter Your Behavior, Prepare You For Heaven And Unleash Uncommon Passion For Life.

Our prayer together...

"Father, use the words of this book as Seeds of greatness planted in the soil of Your people. Remind us of Your *Greatness,* our *Need* for You and the Access You have provided.

Holy Spirit, You are the Source of uncommon joy, uncommon peace and uncommon Wisdom.

Burn these words into our lives like the branding iron on a newborn calf.

Expose every falsehood.

Remove every Enemy.

Change Us Through Your Word.

In Jesus' Name. Amen."

RECOMMENDED BOOKS AND TAPES ON THIS TOPIC

B-01   Wisdom for Winning (228 pages/$10)
B-80   The Greatest Success Habit on Earth (32 pages/$3)
B-100   The Holy Spirit Handbook, Vol. 1 (153 pages/$10)
TS-01   Wisdom for Winning (6 tapes/$30)
TS-29   The Holy Spirit Handbook (6 tapes/$30)

DR. MIKE MURDOCK

1 Has embraced his Assignment to Pursue...Proclaim...and Publish the Wisdom of God to help people achieve their dreams and goals.

2 Began full-time evangelism at the age of 19, which has continued since 1966.

3 Has traveled and spoken to more than 15,000 audiences in 39 countries, including East and West Africa, the Orient and Europe.

4 Noted author of 200 books, including best sellers, *Wisdom for Winning, Dream Seeds* and *The Double Diamond Principle.*

5 Created the popular "Topical Bible" series for Businessmen, Mothers, Fathers, Teenagers; "The One-Minute Pocket Bible" series, and "The Uncommon Life" series.

6 Has composed more than 5,700 songs such as "I Am Blessed," "You Can Make It," "God Rides On Wings Of Love" and "Jesus Just The Mention Of Your Name," recorded by many gospel artists.

7 Is the Founder of The Wisdom Center, in Fort Worth, Texas.

8 Has a weekly television program called *"Wisdom Keys With Mike Murdock."*

9 Has appeared often on TBN, CBN, BET and other television network programs.

10 Has had more than 3,500 accept the call into full-time ministry under his ministry.

THE MINISTRY

1 **Wisdom Books & Literature -** Over 200 best-selling Wisdom Books and 70 Teaching Tape Series.

2 **Church Crusades** - Multitudes are ministered to in crusades and seminars throughout America in "The Uncommon Wisdom Conferences." Known as a man who loves pastors, he has focused on church crusades for 40 years.

3 **Music Ministry** - Millions have been blessed by the anointed songwriting and singing of Mike Murdock, who has made over 15 music albums and CDs available.

4 **Television** - *"Wisdom Keys With Mike Murdock,"* a nationally-syndicated weekly television program features Mike Murdock's teaching and music.

5 **The Wisdom Center** - The Church and Ministry Offices where Dr. Murdock speaks weekly on Wisdom for The Uncommon Life.

6 **Schools of The Holy Spirit** - Mike Murdock hosts Schools of The Holy Spirit in many churches to mentor believers on the Person and companionship of The Holy Spirit.

7 **Schools of Wisdom** - In many major cities Mike Murdock hosts Schools of Wisdom for those who want personalized and advanced training for achieving "The Uncommon Life."

8 **Missionary Ministry** - Dr. Murdock's overseas outreaches to 39 countries have included crusades in East and West Africa, South America and Europe.

DECISION

Will You Accept Jesus As Your Personal Savior Today?

The Bible says, "That if thou shalt confess with thy mouth the Lord Jesus, and shalt believe in thine heart that God hath raised Him from the dead, thou shalt be saved," (Romans 10:9).

Pray this prayer from your heart today!

"Dear Jesus, I believe that You died for me and rose again on the third day. I confess I am a sinner...I need Your love and forgiveness... Come into my heart. Forgive my sins. I receive Your eternal life. Confirm Your love by giving me peace, joy and supernatural love for others. Amen."

Clip and Mail

DR. MIKE MURDOCK

is in tremendous demand as one of the most dynamic speakers in America today.

More than 15,000 audiences in 39 countries have attended his Schools of Wisdom and conferences. Hundreds of invitations come to him from churches, colleges and business corporations. He is a noted author of over 200 books, including the best sellers, *The Leadership Secrets of Jesus* and *Secrets of the Richest Man Who Ever Lived.* Thousands view his weekly television program, *"Wisdom Keys With Mike Murdock."* Many attend his Schools of Wisdom that he hosts in major cities of America.

❏ Yes, Mike! I made a decision to accept Christ as my personal Savior today. Please send me my free gift of your book, *"31 Keys to a New Beginning"* to help me with my new life in Christ. *(B-48)*

NAME   BIRTHDAY

ADDRESS

CITY   STATE   ZIP

PHONE   E-MAIL

Mail form to:
The Wisdom Center • 4051 Denton Hwy. • Ft. Worth, TX 76117
Phone: 1-888-WISDOM-1 (1-817-759-0300)
Website: TheWisdomCenter.tv

JOIN THE

Wisdom Key 3000
TODAY!

Will You Become My Ministry Partner In The Work Of God?

Dear Partner,

God has connected us!

I have asked The Holy Spirit for 3000 Special Partners who will plant a monthly Seed of $58.00 to help me bring the gospel around the world. (58 represents 58 kinds of blessings in the Bible.)

Will you become my monthly Faith Partner in The Wisdom Key 3000? Your monthly Seed of $58.00 is so powerful in helping heal broken lives. When you sow into the work of God, 4 Miracle Harvests are guaranteed in Scripture, Isaiah 58...

▶ Uncommon Health (Isaiah 58)

▶ Uncommon Wisdom For Decision-Making (Isaiah 58)

▶ Uncommon Financial Favor (Isaiah 58)

▶ Uncommon Family Restoration (Isaiah 58)

Your Faith Partner,

Mike Murdock

Unexpected Insurance Check...!

I will share the miracles and blessings of the $58 Seed that wrapped my faith around this month. The insurance company told me the other insurance company did not want to pay the first $500 that I had put out when we were hit. Well this month a restoration check for $500 arrived in the mail.

N.G. NJ

Electric Bill Paid...!

I just wanted to write and thank you for your prayers and to let you know that we have experienced miracles from God. My daughter and son-in-law were behind by $1,000 on their electric bill. They were later informed that their bill had been paid in full. My son had to go to the hospital with no medical insurance. He received a bill for $3,800. A few days later he got another statement with the amount owed marked $0. It had been paid by a charitable organization that operates within the hospital. I'm happy to have made the $58 month pledge and to be one of your Wisdom Key 3000 faith partners.

J. & S. H. IL

Custody Battle Solved...!

We sent in a $58 Seed for half, if not full custody of my husband's children from a previous marriage. We received half custody. Also, $68,000 of child support which was owed was erased.

M. & A. M. WA

Healing...!

My praise report is that I gave a $58 Seed and my health has been improving in my body. I asked you to pray for my lymphatic system and muscles that had broken down and shut down. Every day I feel strength in my legs I haven't felt before and I can tell the difference in my walk, and I am losing weight. I feel my strength coming back.

C. G. VA

Financial Blessing...!

I am 91 years old. I conduct a weekly prayer teaching fellowship at the senior facility where I live. I am so blessed by how God is using you. I can testify to sowing a $58 Seed and receiving $2,000. I was then able to pay the pledge in full for the entire remaining $58 Seeds.

M. G. MI

A New Car...!

I do have a praise report. My last $58 Seed was for a new truck. Well, I'm driving a new Lincoln Navigator. Also I received 2 new students already for my school.

C. D. MN

Unexpected Check...!

Several months ago I was watching your program on TV and I felt I was one who should plant a $58 Seed. On the very day I received written acknowledgement of that Seed, I also received in the mail a very unexpected check for more than $1,400. It was sorely needed at the time.

R. D. MO

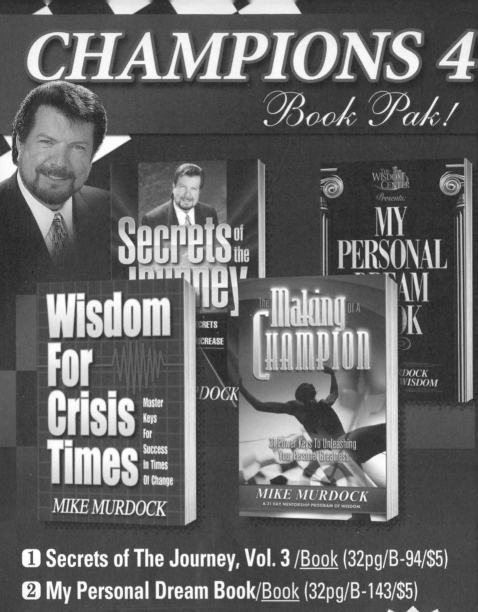

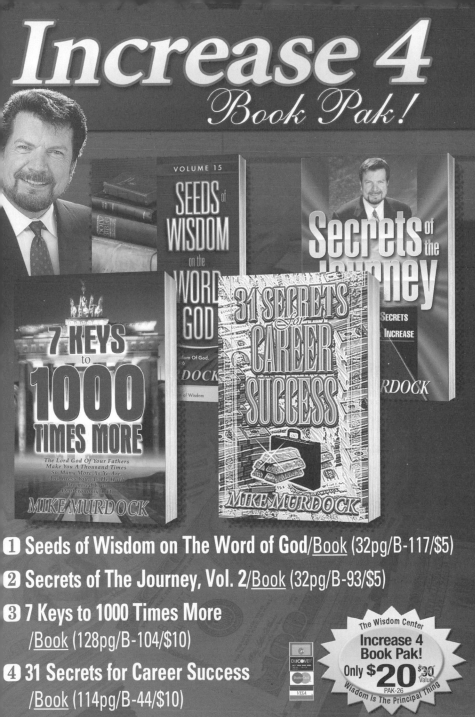

Increase 4 Book Pak!

① Seeds of Wisdom on The Word of God/Book (32pg/B-117/$5)

② Secrets of The Journey, Vol. 2/Book (32pg/B-93/$5)

③ 7 Keys to 1000 Times More
/Book (128pg/B-104/$10)

④ 31 Secrets for Career Success
/Book (114pg/B-44/$10)

The Wisdom Center
Increase 4 Book Pak!
Only $**20** ~~$30~~ Value!
PAK-26
Wisdom Is The Principal Thing

's offer expires December 31st, 2007.   **Each Wisdom Book may be purchased separately if so desired.

Add 10% For S/H

253

Unforgettable Woman 4 Book Pak!

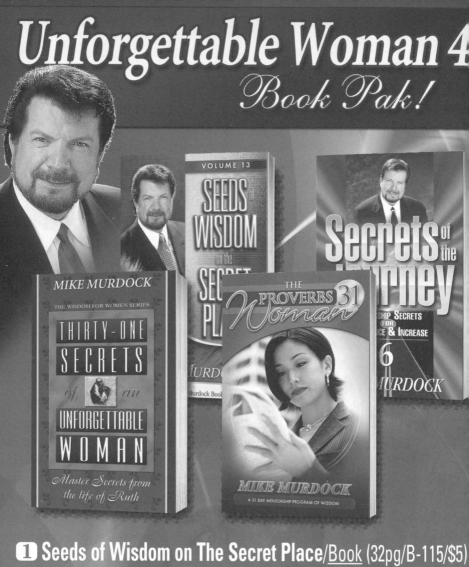

1. **Seeds of Wisdom on The Secret Place**/<u>Book</u> (32pg/B-115/$5)
2. **Secrets of The Journey, Vol. 6**/<u>Book</u> (32pg/B-102/$5)
3. **Thirty-One Secrets of an Unforgettable Woman**/<u>Book</u> (140pg/B-57/$9)
4. **The Proverbs 31 Woman** /<u>Book</u> (70pg/B-49/$7)

The Wisdom Center
Unforgettable Woman 4 Book Pak!
Only $**20** $26 Value
PAK-31
Wisdom Is The Principal Thing

*This offer expires December 31st, 2007.   **Each Wisdom Book may be purchased separately if so desired.

Add 10% For S/H

THE WISDOM CENTER 4051 Denton Highway • Fort Worth, TX 76117

1-888-WISDOM-1
1-817-759-0300

Website:
TheWisdomCenter.tv

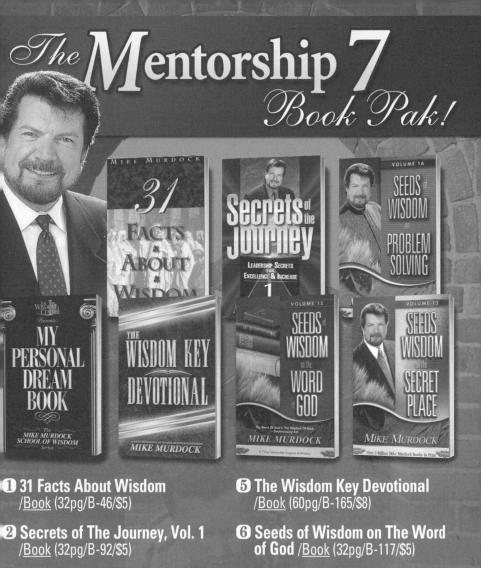

The Mentorship 7 Book Pak!

❶ **31 Facts About Wisdom**
/Book (32pg/B-46/$5)

❷ **Secrets of The Journey, Vol. 1**
/Book (32pg/B-92/$5)

❸ **Seeds of Wisdom on Problem-Solving** /Book (32pg/B-118/$5)

❹ **My Personal Dream Book**
/Book (32pg/B-143/$5)

❺ **The Wisdom Key Devotional**
/Book (60pg/B-165/$8)

❻ **Seeds of Wisdom on The Word of God** /Book (32pg/B-117/$5)

❼ **Seeds of Wisdom on The Secret Place** /Book (32pg/B-115/$5)

All 7 Books For One Great Price!

The Wisdom Center
The Mentorship 7 Book Pak!
Only **$20** $38 Value
PAK-25
Wisdom Is The Principal Thing

Add 10% For S/H

offer expires December 31st, 2007. **Each Wisdom Book may be purchased separately if so desired.*

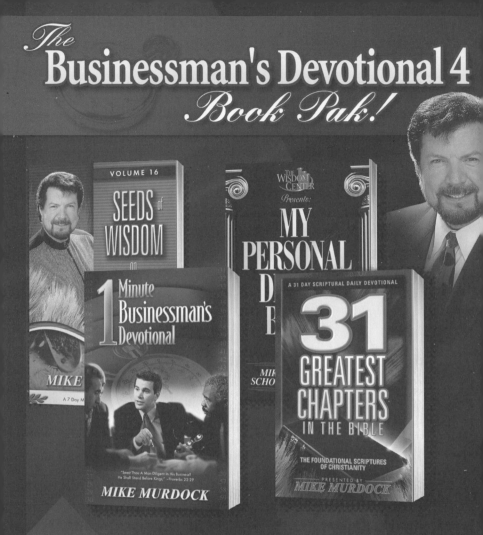